THE
VOLVO DRIVER'S
HIGHWAY CODE

JIM DULLROY

British Library Cataloguing in Publication Data.
A catalogue record for this book is available from the British Library.

ISBN-10: 1-905562-04-7

ISBN-13: 978-1-84426-377-6

Published by Upfront Publishing Ltd

Printed in the UK by Printondemand-worldwide.com

Book sales:
Upfront Publishing Ltd, Graphic House, First Drove, Fengate
Peterborough, Cambridgeshire, PE1 5BJ
Tel:- 01733 352333 Fax:- 01733 352933

www.upfrontpublishing.com

DISCLAIMER

(In case we need it!)

This book has been written with the best of intentions. It is a light-hearted interpretation of the Standard British Highway Code as may be viewed through the eyes of that special breed of motorist, the Volvo Driver. Fundamentally it takes a tongue-in-cheek swipe at the Volvo Driver and his air of invincibility.

In all seriousness, this book is not intended in any way to undermine the principles, requirements and laws laid down in the Highway Code published by HM Stationery Office.

The author or publisher accepts no responsibility whatsoever for any physical, financial or mental damage caused to anyone acting upon the information contained within this book, nor is it our intention to deliberately cause offence.

Having said that, in these politically-correct times if anybody really does take exception to any of the pearls of wisdom contained within we respectfully suggest that he (or she) gets a life!

INTRODUCTION

From the outset let's make one thing perfectly clear. Volvos are, in our opinion, among the finest cars on the road. It's the people that drive them that interest us. So.....

"Bloody Volvo Drivers!" How many times have you heard that when you've been out and about on the roads? It's an expression we're hearing more and more and it's made me curious. Just ask around the motoring world and it seems that Volvo Drivers are becoming social outcasts. But why? What do Volvo Drivers do that the majority of other drivers don't do? Apart, that is, from driving Volvos. Why do they attract such negative publicity? There just had to be a reason for it. And then it dawned. There isn't any particular reason - it was always thus. Volvo Drivers have always been held in low esteem. It's been an accepted way of life for years and it's not about to change now.

30 years ago Volvos seemed to be the exclusive property of the green wellie brigade. Anybody that owned one was labelled as a reliable, but dull, plodder who matched their reliable, but dull, cars. Volvos were built like tanks, never broke down, but wouldn't break land speed records or win any design awards either. The cars were huge; you could use one to move house - in one trip. Now fast forward to today and the picture has changed dramatically. Those reliable chaps at Volvo have given their cars a complete make-over. Gone are the wannabee hearses and in their place a whole range of high performance motors that attract a different type of client. For green wellie brigade now read would-be boy racer brigade. God forbid, but the Corporate world is now allocating Volvos to their reps as company cars, so the Volvo Driver attracts abuse from a wider quarter. *"Bloody Volvo Drivers! Think they own the road"* - as another V40 hurtles past them.

Now you may ask *"What's the big deal?"* Well, I have a confession to make. I am a Bloody Volvo Driver. I own a Volvo. Always have. In fact until recently my wife owned one as well. I drive them because I like them, I drive them because I can afford them, and I drive them because I happen to believe that they are the best car in their class. My choice. And as a Volvo Driver I've had to endure this stigma for years. Suffering in silence. But now enough is enough. It's time to come out of the closet and tell all. You see, there's a good reason why we Volvo Drivers think we own the road. It's because *we do.* We always have, and in this book I shall open to the world the hitherto closely-guarded philosophies and principles that are drummed into us from the minute we drive our first Volvo.

Volvo Drivers are a special breed. We *do* own the road, We're taught to. Those of you lesser mortals that think that *you* own the road are extremely irritating to those of us that actually *do.* In fact one of the best kept secrets in motoring is that Volvo Drivers actually have their own Highway Code and my purpose in writing this book is to reveal exactly what this Highway Code is.

So follow me as we open the pages of the *Volvo Drivers' Highway Code* and you will get to know what really makes the Volvo Driver tick. In this book you will learn the basic roadcraft techniques that the Volvo Driver is taught. You will acquire the skills necessary to make the roads your own personal domain. You can learn how to put the Company Rep, Boy Racer and other assorted hooligans in their place; how to get your own back on the drivers of tractors, trucks and juggernauts; how to deal with the Sunday Driver, Del-Boy 3-Wheelers and drivers of the fairer sex; how to take on and survive the manic attentions of White Van Man. You will be able to master the techniques for frightening Learner Drivers to death, and handling the Curse of the Caravan. You can refine your interpretation of what you can and can't do on Britain's roads to your own advantage. Learn how to drive to the maximum annoyance of everybody else, and how to induce bug-eyed road rage by using no more than a single finger.

Finally, you will gain a deeper appreciation of that special relationship that exists between the Volvo Driver and Mr Plod the Policeman.

Our Highway Code is divided into two main sections; getting to understand the other creatures that may want to share your road with you, and the various skills involved in driving your Volvo and tackling the road network in general. At the end of the book is a reference guide containing a selection of hand signals which can be used to communicate with other road users, and road signs that you may well encounter on your travels. This is followed by a very useful glossary where we explain some of the more technical terms and expressions used in this book.

Enjoy your journey!

Jim Dullroy
©2005

CONTENTS

CONTENTS (continued)

CONTENTS (continued)

CONTENTS (continued)

(....continued)

CONTENTS (continued)

Part A: GET TO KNOW THE OPPOSITION
(other road users)

First, a sobering thought. Because, as a Volvo Driver, you own the road you are entitled to feel that the highways exist for your exclusive use. However, there are millions of other car drivers who, not having had the benefit of Volvo Awareness Training, think that they also have the right to use the road. Not to mention all the other species that you can find on the public highway at one time or another. And there's upwards of a quarter of a million miles of this highway in the UK for them to use.

So you need to know what you're up against. You will need to look at each species of road user, classify them, assess them and then decide what action you would need to take to make the name "Volvo" synonymous with "respect". So let's start off by looking in detail at the opposition, in ascending evolutionary order:

1.   ANIMALS (yes, animals):

It is a disturbing thought for any motorist but animals (i.e. species lower than humans, and *much* lower than Volvo Drivers) do occasionally use the road, intentionally or otherwise. In some cases the law actually allows them to. These animals can vary from a solitary hedgehog to a full herd of cattle. So how should the Volvo Driver tackle these intrusions into his road space?

1.1   Hedgehogs - These mini-animals have absolutely no concept of road sense. They feel that they have the right to *cross* the road just as you're driving *along* it. If you spot one of these creatures you should show due tolerance and take avoiding action if possible. Not only will you enhance your familiar self-righteous glow, but if you don't you'll find that it's a devil of a job having to dig them out of the treads of your tyres afterwards.

12

1.2   Dogs off the leash - Illegal and downright dangerous. Stray dogs can cause havoc on the road. Encountering one may not only cause you to slow down or swerve but might actually make you stop to avoid denting your Volvo. This must not be tolerated. Apprehend the dog, ascertain its address from its collar and report matters to the police. They will appreciate the opportunity of a break from filling in their endless forms to get their teeth into a proper crime. And with any luck the dog's owner will not find out where you live and pay you a visit in the small hours to discuss your views on animal welfare.

1.3   Horses - Horses can generally be found cluttering up the roads in two ways:

> 1.   *Horses with saddles and riders* - the selfishness of some horse riders is astounding. Why, when they can canter blissfully through fields and trot along bridle paths made specially for them, do they insist on using the road - *your* road? And when they do, they are usually two abreast just to make sure you, or anybody else for that matter, can't get past. You will need to play safe so there's not much you can do but wait until you have the room to pass safely. Perish the thought that you should creep up behind one of them and toot your horn. At best you are likely to end up on the receiving end of a shower of fertiliser for your roses; at worst you may make the horse bolt for it which could cause untold damage to your Volvo.

> 2.   *Horses pulling carts or caravans* - sometimes, when the gods have really got it in for you, you will round a bend to meet a horse trotting along quite happily pulling a cart or even a rustic type of caravan, and completely blocking your path in the process. Fortunately there's not too many of them around these days but the ones you do find tend to fall into three categories:

(1)   Drays - usually seen in the vicinity of traditional breweries in the north of England.

(2)   The family horse-and-cart - you can still occasionally spot these quaint contraptions in some villages or out in the country, and where you will often find that the approximate age of the "driver" is twelve.

(3)   Horse-drawn caravans - either New Age Travellers or Romany-type caravans. The former are usually to be found amongst their very own rubbish tips in countryside beauty spots; the latter hired out to nerd families seeking the alternative holiday.

Just as before, your options are limited and you will need to wait for an appropriate moment before overtaking. A suitable location would be as you approach a side street with a "No Entry" sign. Do try and resist the temptation to sound your horn as you roar past. A horse-and-cart in full flight going the wrong way up a one-way street may conjure up hilarious images but in reality they can cause untold havoc. And who knows, there may be another Volvo Driver coming the other way.

1.4   Cattle - It is a well-known fact that farmers take great delight in cluttering up country roads with herds of sheep or cows, usually the one you happen to be driving along at the time and when you're running late. To add insult to injury the farmer can often be found directing operations to the cow-hands from the safety and comfort of **_his_** Volvo estate as it crawls up the road at the front of the herd. As a fellow Volvo Driver you know he will appreciate your predicament. He will therefore fully understand when you blast your horn, causing a stampede in all directions and further delays while the errant cattle are rounded up. Alternatively, if the farmer fails to clear a path through for you just nudge your way through. Once safely through you will then have to negotiate the obstacle of the farmer himself sat in his

Volvo, and you will need to remind him of his social responsibilities in letting herds of cattle loose on the Queen's highway and what does he intend to do about it? You should subsequently find that only a few traces of manure will remain on your Volvo after its seventh trip through the car wash.

2.   PEDESTRIANS:

Unbelievably, you will often find pedestrians actually venturing into the road that has been set aside for your personal use. There are many types of pedestrian and the main ones you are likely to come across are listed below together with the recommended action you should take to remind these upstarts of the perils of straying into Volvo territory. At this point you should always keep in mind one of the fundamental laws of the Volvo Driver:

"So many pedestrians. So little time"

2.1   Pedestrians on pavements and crossings - This is explained in more detail in section 18.11.

2.2   Jaywalkers - There are two types of jaywalker; the quick and the dead. If you are unfortunate enough to encounter one of these help the offender to make up his (or her) mind which category they belong to. Gliding noiselessly right up behind them and blasting your horn has proved quite effective and usually results in the offender rising vertically into the air and having to divert home for a change of underwear.

2.3   Joggers - Unmistakable by their purple features and heaving torsos these sad individuals are prime candidates for the local Cardiac Unit as they wheeze along the public thoroughfares in the mistaken belief that they are actually doing themselves some good. Because, usually, they are moving faster than your average pedestrian joggers require a clear path, and the pavement is littered with loitering people. So they take to the road. Your road. And in doing so they assume that they have the right to take up half the width of your side of the road. Remind them of their position in life by waiting until you find a large puddle - a deep one - and when the joggers are alongside it drive through it at speed. They will be glad of the cooling effect of all that muddy water after their exertions and with any luck your brakes may have dried out before your next emergency stop - around the next bend where you meet another set of joggers, friends of the ones you've just baptised.

2.4   Hitch-hikers - You should regard these creatures as nothing more than parasites and ignore them. You have to pay your way in this life and so should they. By and large hitch-hikers tend to be a scruffy lot that don't make too many appointments with a bar of soap. They also have an unappealing tendency to wear the same clothes for weeks on end. It therefore goes without saying that you will not want to contaminate your Volvo's plush upholstery with these grubby specimens. If you see a hitch-hiker just drive on with that familiar smug expression of superiority. Alternatively you may want to treat them to an overdue wash if they happen to be standing near a puddle *(see Joggers, previous section)*.

2.5   Pedestrians en masse - If jaywalking pedestrians wandering into your road wasn't bad enough occasionally you will find that they deliberately congregate in herds to block up the entire highway. These social gatherings are known by a variety of guises, the most popular being "Fun Runs" or "Protest Marches". Unlike sheep or cattle (see previous sections) blasting your horn won't make them disperse. As you will be heavily outnumbered you would be wise to let discretion be the better part of valour on this occasion and seek an alternative route, particularly as these gatherings tend to attract dozens of Old Bill. No point in setting yourself up.

2.6 Pedestrians on wheels - There have been recent sightings in London and other city centres of some pedestrians ascending to the next evolutionary level in order for them to move around that bit quicker. They do this by attaching wheels to their footwear in the form of roller-blades, and then take to the roads. Not the pavements; the roads. They hurl themselves along like Olympic speed-skaters, arms flailing as they weave in and out of the traffic. Some have even been seen doing a Frank Spencer impression when they grab hold of a car or a bus and let themselves get pulled along. Of course, they won't have realised it at first but they have made one huge mistake - taking to the roads in the first place. This is Volvo territory. Also, since speed-skaters have yet to become a protected species under the Standard Highway Code they will not have the immunity from the Volvo Driver that, say, a cyclist enjoys (see next section). They must therefore be taught that the roads are dangerous places and who better to administer this lesson than the Volvo Driver? Wait until you spy a speed-skater in the street and cruise around. Kerb-crawl if you have to. Eventually he or she will latch on to your Volvo for a free ride. Then proceed to put the Volvo through its paces, and if you are fortunate enough to be driving a T5 so much the better. He (or she) will be hanging on to the back of your car like grim death as realisation dawns that roller-blading down the A1 is probably not a good idea. However, it is recommended that you stop short of actually performing a handbrake turn, however tempting it may be. Whip-lashing a speed-skater into orbit may not be viewed favourably by the magistrates.

3.   CYCLISTS:

To the Volvo Driver cyclists are way, way down the evolutionary scale among road users, and are generally considered to be a pain in the big ends. In fact there is a school of thought, popular among motorists, that cyclists need to be raised up on two wheels to avoid dragging their knuckles along the street.

What endears cyclists to the Volvo Driver is that they use his road with official consent, but with no responsibilities whatsoever. They are a breed apart, unpredictable and downright dangerous to the motorist but are perceived to be role models by the politically correct conservationists and environmental freaks that infest our local Town Halls. In predictable fashion cyclists are positively encouraged to clog up the roads to discourage the motorist. They are free from the burdens of road tax and insurance that the rest of us have to pay, and to add insult to injury they are provided with their own gaily coloured special lanes on the roads for their exclusive use. Naturally these cycle lanes are at their most prevalent on the busiest main roads that are already too narrow to cope with today's volume of traffic, so the width of the road is reduced still further for the Volvo Driver that actually pays to use it. Needless to say, straying into one of these cycle lanes with your Volvo makes you fair game for Mr Plod in his jam sandwich, and severe punishment awaits. *(See also section 22 on Road Works for further information on coloured cycle lanes).*

Cyclists ride with impunity, committing traffic offences which would see the rest of us in the nick. They jump red lights, go the wrong way up one-way streets, and when the mood takes them think nothing of riding on the pavements. In fact riding on pavements is positively encouraged in some of the more progressive towns where the authorities have actually painted cycle lanes *on* the pavements, presumably as a contributory measure to reducing the number of elderly citizens that might end up in their care.

As with cars (see later) there are many types of cyclist. During a typical journey in your Volvo why not play "I-Spy" and see how many of the following you can spot :

> 1.   *The Shy, Retiring Type* - these nurse a hidden guilt complex about being a cyclist, so to avoid being identified they cycle only at night - without lights.

2.   *The Pavement Artist* - why cycle on busy roads when you can ride your bike on the pavement, cycle lanes or no cycle lanes? Much more fun scattering old ladies in all directions.

3.   *The Bucking Bronco* - these are the younger cyclists who delight in rearing up on the back wheel to see how far they can get, one-handed, unicycle-style. (The can of lager for the other hand is optional).

4.   *The Dodderer* - jaywalkers on wheels. These are the older generation (much older) riding bikes straight out of the post-war era. They cycle at walking pace, handlebars swinging from side to side, making it virtually impossible to overtake them on a narrow road.

5.   *The Lycra Sausage Dogs* - you've seen them; the health freaks with their ciabatta-and-rocket-salad-nourished torsos poured into one of those appalling lycra body stockings that finish just above the knee. The only way you can tell the men from the women is that the women usually have the hairier legs. Off they go bursting with energy, breaking the law by exceeding the speed limit and riding three abreast, and generally offering patronising abuse to any Volvo Driver who has the temerity to suggest that they might like to observe the fundamental principles of the Highway Code (as distinct from the *Volvo Driver's Highway Code*) and stay within the law. In response, keeping a small supply of tacks or drawing pins in your glove box is recommended. In the unfortunate event that they should be accidentally scattered in their path it has been reported that the results can be quite mirth-provoking while you, of course, would be long gone and free from any slanderous accusations.

6.   *The Health Freak Rallies* - these are the Lycra Sausage Dogs en masse where dozens of them take to the road, your

19

road, and proceed to impede every law-abiding and tax-paying road user - not just Volvos. The best course of action here is the tacks mentioned previously, but more of them.

Note of Caution: Just be very careful that, should any of these tacks do become scattered in their paths, none of them bounce off the bikes and land under your Volvo. You may or may not want every cyclist in the vicinity standing around wetting themselves with laughter while *you* have to change *your* wheel in your best suit - and then realise you've left the locking wheel nut adapter which is needed to get the wheel off back in your garage.

7.   *Tweedledum and Tweedledee* - a multiple variation of the Dodderer, only younger. Side by side they amble along on that narrow, winding country road. They just can't bear to be separated as they giggle and chatter amongst themselves, completely oblivious to the Volvo six inches behind them.

Back on the subject of local councils, some of the more liberal public bodies have taken the encouragement of cyclists to extremes. Whole areas of towns have been designated as Apache-style reservations for as many cyclists as they can cram in, and the Volvo Driver becomes hopelessly outnumbered as these two-wheeled gremlins go on the attack with official blessing. If you think this is an exaggeration, the author has two words for you: *Visit Cambridge* (and go by train).

4.   MOTORCYCLISTS:

This is another breed that think that the official Highway Code, motoring bye-laws and other regulations only apply to vehicles with four wheels or more. Motorcycles range in size from the motorised scooters used for pizza deliveries to the huge gleaming Japanese and German mean machines. The driving habits of the motorcyclist are somewhat reminiscent of the cyclist; i.e. weaving through lanes of traffic, hogging the centre of the lane that you're driving in, etc, etc. They also know exactly how to wind the Volvo Driver up, for example:

- They expect the best of both worlds. They like to be treated as a 2-wheeler for purposes of road tax and getting away with cyclist-type tricks and manoeuvres, but demand parity with a car when it comes to parking. Take a typical scenario in ASDA's car park (note the words **car** park and not **motorcycle** park). One of the fundamental laws of parking *(see section 21)* states that any car parking space that could comfortably hold two or even three motorbikes will only ever be occupied by one - while the Volvo Driver circles endlessly around looking for a space that he can squeeze into.

- They will sit in the blind spot in your wing mirror, waiting for an opportunity to overtake. When it is totally unsafe to do so (for example, approaching the brow of a hill, blind bend, or seeing you pull out to overtake the vehicle in front of you) they will shoot past you at full throttle and disappear up the inside of the car in front of you. Should you get the opportunity to catch up with him, for example at the next contraflow or even pulled off the road at a Greasy Spoon, attempt to engage him in conversation regarding his obligations to other road users, suggesting the deference that is due to the Volvo Driver. It is at this point that he removes his helmet and closer inspection of both him and his motorbike reveals that he is in fact a great big hairy tattooed Hell's Angel. It is also at this point that you realise that Hell's Angels never travel alone, as the rest of the chapter arrive on the scene to join in the dialogue. Fortunately you will still have your RAC Membership number on you and arranging for replacement windscreen wipers and wing mirrors shouldn't present too much of a problem.

5.   CARS (and the people who drive them):

There are umpteen million cars on British roads and consequently they represent by far the most common type of adversary that the Volvo Driver has to face.

There are many varieties of car but the Volvo Driver will classify them according to the nature of the driver and the particular hazards that each brings to the road. So, as we did for cyclists in section 3, let's play "I-Spy" and see how many of the following different types of car driver you can spot during an average journey in your Volvo, and what action you may need to take in each case:

5.1   Ordinary cars that are not Volvos - These are very simple to classify; those cheaper than your Volvo and those more expensive than your Volvo. You should treat them as follows:

> 1.   *Cars cheaper than your Volvo* - these are obviously inferior vehicles and no respect whatsoever should be given to them. They are to be derided and despised.

> *Note:* Should you be uncertain there is one sure way to tell if a car is of the cheaper variety. On a clear day listen very carefully - you will be able to hear the gentle sound of it rusting.

> 2.   *Cars more expensive than your Volvo* - these are obviously pretentious and consider themselves to be the prima donnas of the road. As such they will be excessively ostentatious and driven by those who delude themselves that the roads actually belong to *them*. When encountering one of these vehicles there is no need for any confrontation, challenges or trials of one-upmanship. They should simply be ignored.

5.2   Del-Boy 3-Wheelers - These amusing vehicles, immortalised in *"Only Fools and Horses"*, have been likened to mobilised sewing machines with lids on. However, they should not be underestimated. Here are some interesting, but little-known, facts about the Del-Boy 3-Wheeler which the Volvo Driver would do well to take seriously, difficult as that may be to comprehend:

- They are capable of quite extraordinary speeds. Sightings of these vehicles doing 90 mph have been reported, though subsequent scientific studies have concluded that this could only be achieved by getting caught in the slipstream of a T5.

- They were originally built for drivers over the age of 70 who would be unlikely to do any more than potter about quite happily at 20 mph, wearing their obligatory flat caps. Which is why these vehicles were originally christened as "the skateboard of the un-dead".

- In the unfortunate event of a prang there would be no need for the services of a breakdown truck to remove the damaged 3-Wheeler. This can be done quite adequately with a dustpan and brush.

- There have been sightings of them towing a caravan. Either that, or the caravan was pushing the 3-Wheeler. Difficult to tell.

- They are cheap and easy to service. Most spare parts can be bought at any reputable stationers selling rubber bands and glue-sticks.

- They are environmentally friendly. At the end of their useful life those metal bits of each 3-Wheeler that have not rusted away can be recycled as kitchen foil.

5.3   Boy Racers - Of all the motoring types that the Volvo Driver has to contend with the Boy Racer is the most irritating. These adolescent lunatics actually aspire to be faster and better than the Volvo Driver who is viewed with derision and pity. Respect? They don't know the meaning of the word.

You can't mistake them. Souped-up old saloon, musical car horn, giant chrome exhaust with a hole in it for that extra "throaty" effect, green tinted name-strips for the top of the windscreen, go-faster stripes, wheels three sizes too big for the car, and a sound system that would do credit to the Albert Hall, played of course at full volume with the windows down. It screams up behind you from nowhere, tailgates you while swerving from side to side, deciding whether to overtake or undertake, eventually overtakes at full revs in second gear on a blind bend and roars off on it's next lap of dishonour.

Occasionally Boy Racer thinks it would be fun to challenge the Volvo Driver to a race in order to enhance his street cred. Don't disappoint him, but do allow yourself to choose the weapons, and the time and place for the forthcoming duel. Your vehicle should be a T5, nothing less, and preferably with the badge removed so that Boy Racer isn't one hundred percent sure what he's up against. Now play dirty. Select a location that you know has hidden speed cameras and, more importantly, where they are. And off you go. The T5 will, of course, leave Boy Racer standing. Then gradually ease off the gas and let him overtake. He will be so puffed up thinking he's come out on top he probably won't even notice the trail of engine components that he's leaving behind him in the road. And if he does make it to the speed cameras he's bang to rights anyway. You, in the meantime, will have slowed to a law-abiding speed, blissfully unaware of that extra set of speed cameras that they put up only last week just after where you started the race.

5.4   Company Reps - You can spot them a mile off. Estate cars packed full of boxes and the tell-tale jacket and shirts swinging from a coathanger hooked above the nearside rear window. Mobile phone clamped to his ear. Having been given unrealistic appointment schedules the Company Rep attempts to break the land speed record in his standard issue 1.6 Mondeo / Vectra / whatever. The general demeanour and attitude to other road users makes the Rep ideally suited to drive a Volvo, and sightings of Reps driving S40's have actually been recorded.

The parts of the Company Rep's car which wear out the quickest are the horn and headlamp flasher which are in constant use to alert other motorists of his existence. Should you be driving your Volvo along the motorway in the lane reserved for Volvos, i.e. the outside, and you encounter the Company Rep behind you then stay where you are. You are in the right and these impatient fools must be taught good manners. If he persists in tailgating you then gradually slow down. This will be met with much flashing of headlights, and possibly fist-waving or even impolite hand signals, and should drive him to seek the illegal alternative manoeuvre of roaring past you on the inside. At this point, *you* move over to the middle or inside lane which, of course, you are perfectly entitled to do. If he is already in the process of carving you up on the inside he will be faced with the choice of either braking violently, thereby showering him with all the boxes in the back of his car, being pushed off the road altogether, or driving into you. In the latter case you will both need to stop. This will provide you with the opportunity of discussing the merits of his driving skills, and you should find that most of the bruising will fade within a week or so.

5.5   Sunday Drivers - The Volvo Driver has many obstacles to overcome in his constant quest for motoring superiority, and among the most annoying is the *Great British Sunday Driver*. Actually they can emerge at any time during the weekend but the effect is always the same. The car stays in the garage all week and is brought out at weekends for a special treat. Every weekend the car is meticulously cleaned, whether it needs it or not, polished, tyre pressures checked, oil level checked, and all this regardless of the fact that it only clocks up about 100 miles a week. Sunday Driver loads the wife into the car, together with picnic requisites, maps and assorted essentials, and proceeds to take to the road. Your road. The one you have chosen to be on as you have a busy day in front of you. He won't use dual carriageways, preferring the scenic route of country roads where it's almost impossible to overtake. So he ambles along at 40 mph, completely oblivious to the stream of traffic building up behind him.

The more professional Sunday Driver wears a special uniform consisting of a flat cap, collar and tie and sometimes string-backed gloves, and is usually long past retirement age which means he now also qualifies as an Elderly Driver *(see section 15.4)*. Anyway, whatever his perceived age you do need to ensure that Sunday Driver is properly briefed regarding his obligations to other road users and especially the Volvo Driver. You will, eventually, be able to overtake him. When you do try and resist the temptation to toot your horn and offer one of the many hand signals that form such an essential part of the Volvo Driver's armoury. Much better to discreetly draw up alongside him when you finally get the chance, for example at traffic lights, wind the window down and engage him in social pleasantries. Ask, for example, whether he would like your help in finding third gear, or suggest that if he goes any slower it may be more appropriate if he got out and milked it.

**5.6   Learner Drivers - **Having not passed their driving test the Learner Driver is blissfully unaware of the Volvo Driver, the intimidation that he brings to the road, and therefore the respect that is due. At the time of publication, to its everlasting discredit the standard Highway Code has not included a specific section on the superiority of the Volvo Driver, so it is safe to assume that the Learner Driver won't learn any better from the driving instructor either. The Learner Driver will be trained in blind obedience to all aspects of the law i.e. how to be a one-man traffic jam. The Volvo Driver is experienced and therefore has a duty to pass on his knowledge of roadcraft to the learner, and what better way to achieve this than through practical exercises? This is sometimes known as the "Baptism of Fire" and will toughen them up for the challenges that lie in wait once they pass their test. You will need to psyche them out; play mind games with them to see how easy it is to unsettle them. They will learn from it, and will thank you for it.

Find a Learner Driver and creep up behind him (or better still, her). Stay there for three to four minutes at a steady 28 mph, passing up all opportunities to overtake. He (or she) will spend more time nervously looking in the rear view mirror than they will out of the windscreen, prompting much chastisement from the instructor. This will make them worse and unsettle him (or her) even more. Now overtake and settle down to a nice steady 28 mph in front of them (Learner plus instructor) for another couple of miles. The Learner will now be transfixed by the rear end of your Volvo. Now find a roundabout and signal right, but go all the way round and back up the same road you just left. By this time Learner Driver plus instructor will have gone straight on and you will now be behind them again. Maintain your speed behind them, again ignoring overtaking opportunities, then without warning overtake them and settle down to a nice steady 28 mph again. Glance in your rear view mirror to see if Learner Driver has been reduced to a gibbering wreck. If he / she has then they will never make it as a driver and you will have performed a valuable service for the Volvo Owners Club in keeping another inadequate off the road.

A sobering thought - Even Volvo Drivers started life as Learner Drivers but of course in our day it was different.

5.7   Women Drivers - There is a school of thought that if God had wanted women to drive cars He would have given them brains and a sense of direction. But women **_are_** allowed to drive cars and in doing so they bring with them a whole new dimension of grief for the Volvo Driver. In fact, there appears to be an alarming increase in the number of ladies who actually aspire to be Volvo Drivers themselves.

Now, the knee-jerk reaction to this is to send your driving licence back to the DVLA and enter a monastery but when the ability to think clearly returns you will find that things may, after all, not be quite so bad as they first seemed. You will realise that it is highly unlikely that the female of the species would possess sufficient of the qualities necessary to be a fully paid-up Volvo Driver; i.e. an overwhelming sense of superiority, total lack of sensitivity, zero tolerance threshold, and a large helping of bloody-mindedness. These qualities are essential in maintaining the differential between the Volvo Driver and the rest of the plebs on the road. And then you start to think about the finer points of owning and driving a Volvo, and the challenges that a woman Volvo Driver would face. For example, Volvo Drivers are required to:

- park the car. This will inevitably involve use of reverse gear; you know - the one that makes the car go backwards.

- put petrol in the car, and the right petrol for the car at that. Volvo diesels tend not to maximise their performance on a tankful of unleaded.

- check the engine oil level once in a while. If it needs topping up the oil is poured into the special filler nozzle provided for that purpose and not dripped slowly down the dipstick.

- keep the cooling system topped up with water. When required, water should be poured into the container provided for that purpose, and not into the brake fluid reservoir.

- keep the windscreen washer bottle filled with water and a dash of washing-up liquid. This should be done carefully with a jug and not with a hose at full blast.

- ensure that the rear view mirror is aligned to observe the traffic behind. It should ***not*** be lined up for checking eye-liner and lipstick for possible refurbishment.

- know their left from their right, and be able to read a map. The black lines on an Ordnance Survey map look lovely and straight but Volvos cannot travel along them - these are railway lines.

- keep the car clean, at least so that you can see through the windscreen. This may involve a visit to the car wash. In this event, the car should not be driven ***through*** the car wash but kept stationary while the mobile washer machine does its job. Sunroofs or windows should ***not*** be kept ajar to let in the fresh air since they will also let in 50 gallons of diluted industrial detergent, laying waste to umpteen pounds worth of hair styling and cosmetic treatments as well as the interior of the car.

- occasionally change a wheel; you know - when the tyre goes flat. This is one motoring task that is absolutely guaranteed to sort the men from the boys - or even the ladies. It must be admitted that sightings have been reported of some ladies actually having a go at this, even at the risk of chipping their nail varnish, and this initiative is to be applauded. Unfortunately most will stand demurely and helplessly by the side of the road, one leg flashed in the expectation that a chivalrous male driver will take pity on her and stop and do the job for her. And this in the age of sexual equality and female liberation, too. However, they reckon without the Volvo Driver. Apart from the fact that any such act of chivalry will lead to immediate expulsion from the Volvo Owners Club in disgrace, most Volvo Drivers do not find white cellulite all that attractive.

It is acknowledged, however, that there will be periods (no pun intended) when a lady's general demeanour comes close to satisfying the standards required to be a Volvo Driver. Usually every fourth week.

5.8   Taxis - Taxis should be regarded by the Volvo Driver as tightly-wrapped packages of road rage just waiting to happen. Inherently unstable in their make-up, the taxi driver is required to get from A to B in the fastest possible time in order to free himself up that bit quicker for the next fare. This has a detrimental effect on their driving skills as they come to regard any motorist who doesn't drive in the same way as fair game to be hooted at, flashed and cursed repeatedly. They would, in fact, make ideal Volvo Drivers.

You will find that there are two types of taxi; the licenced hackney cab and the minicab:

> 1.   *Hackney Cabs* - these are the taxis that ply their trade at locations such as railway stations and airports. They rely on the punters being a captive market, and charge accordingly. They are also very protective of their territories and make it their mission in life to terrorise any motorist who they may suspect of being an undercover taxi driver. They are easily identified by a plate fixed on the rear of the cab which bears their hackney licence number.

> 2.   *Minicabs* - these are the taxi firms for private hire. Though their rates are usually cheaper than the hackney cabs, you do stand a much better chance of getting ripped off, particularly if you find yourself in a strange town or city. Minicab drivers also tend to be a special breed and their vehicles are easily identified by the dents and scratches on the car's bodywork, caused through driving by touch rather than judgement and underlining the taxi driver's generally appalling driving standards.

It is really beneath you to mess with the taxi driver. Not only are they always in the right but they tend to colonise with other taxi drivers and are able to call up reinforcements at very short notice to outnumber and intimidate you.

5.9   Police Cars - Forget it. This is one battle you're never going to win. Know your limitations and accept you've been beaten by the better man, if only for the fact that the police car is also likely to be a Volvo, and with your luck a T5, and it's always going to be marginally faster than yours. It is unwise to challenge a T5 jam sandwich to a duel of driving skills at high speed. Even if you win they will cheat and call up reinforcements and you will not only lose the race but probably your driving licence as well. This could seriously impair your personal campaign to establish Volvo Drivers at the forefront of global motoring.

5.10   Unmarked Police Cars - Jam sandwiches in plain clothes - the dirtiest trick of all. This lot are in a class of their own and are perhaps the sneakiest category of motorist that the Volvo Driver will ever have to contend with. They are dedicated to preventing the Volvo Driver from going about his lawful business at unlawful speeds.

While Police Authorities plead poverty and lack of "resources", closing down rural police stations, taking bobbies off the beat, and generally giving the green light to the ungodly they always seem to find the "resources" to buy souped-up expensive foreign motors and stuff them full of thousands of pounds' worth of speed monitoring devices, video recorders and the latest hi-tech global navigation systems, for the express purpose of nailing hapless motorists doing 5 mph over the speed limit on a clear road on a sunny day. This is most prevalent in those parts of the country which, strangely, also have the highest rates of unsolved burglaries, car thefts and other crimes. The Volvo Driver is therefore entitled to feel a little perplexed at these strange social priorities and should you fall foul of an unmarked car you should politely ask the officers who have pulled you over why this is so. Stand up for your rights and be dignified. Ask why they feel the need to drive incognito. Emphasise that, during the last war, spies masquerading as civilians were shot. Tell them that, in your opinion, the *Volvo Driver's Highway Code* has made an error in classification and that on the evolutionary scale with other road users the unmarked police car ranks at the beginning, somewhere below hedgehogs, but with the essential difference that with hedgehogs the pricks are on the outside.

Consider your subsequent court appearance as a rich and varied learning experience and performing a much-needed public service, standing up for the millions of persecuted motorists on Britain's roads, and that it took a Volvo Driver to do it. Ensure that your lawyer is fully briefed of these facts.

(See also section 23 which describes other circumstances in which the Volvo Driver may encounter Mr Plod the Policeman).

6.   CARAVANS:

It is a widely held view among Volvo Drivers that they will vote for the first political party that includes within its manifesto proposals to tax these appalling contraptions off the road. Caravans are quite simply an anti-social menace and contribute absolutely zilch to the quality of the Volvo Driver's motoring environment. Quite the reverse, in fact. They cause the towing vehicle to use more fuel, adding to environmental pollution, and generally do their best to jam up the entire road network between March and October. Presumably they hibernate for the winter. Roads to the coast, country picnic areas and campsites are favourite, and whichever road it is it will always be the one you happen to be driving along in your Volvo.

Caravans are also inherently unstable and when towed at speed snake across the road making overtaking on a single lane road a definitely dicey business - if you manage to get past at all. The towing car will also be equipped with large elongated wing mirrors so that the driver can watch in amusement as miles of traffic build up behind him. This is nothing more than a red rag to a bull to the Volvo Driver, especially when in he's in a hurry which is usually the case. Out-of-character road rage can strike, and undue risks can be taken. Of course, the Volvo Driver cannot be held responsible for his actions considering the provocation to which he has been subjected, and irrational things start to happen. For example, if you are fortunate (and astute) enough to eventually overtake a caravan tuck yourself right in front and rapidly switch your rear fog lights on and off. This will be interpreted as sudden braking lights to the caravan driver who will then proceed to slam on his brakes. The resulting jack-knife is a joy for the Volvo Driver to behold in his rear view mirror - just as a Volvo Driver coming the other way does exactly the same thing. It is at this point that you realise that your RAC membership expired last week and that you will now have to foot the bill for being pulled out of the hedgerows.

A sobering thought - reported sightings of a Volvo pulling a caravan are usually attributed to hallucinations brought about by the fatigue of too much driving. There can be no other reasonable explanation for this strange phenomenon.

7.   WHITE VAN MAN:

These are generically no more than Boy Racers with delusions of grandeur brought on by the size of the vehicles that they drive. These are the Transits, Mercedes and other vans driven, for want of a better word, by couriers, delivery contractors, plumbers, engineers, builders merchants, pop bands, to name but a few. They try and take as few prisoners as possible and therefore must be considered as adversaries - and inferior ones at that. They have two distinguishing features that the Volvo Driver must recognise to enable him to effectively plan for the inevitable duel that will ensue if you give White Van Man half the chance:

(1)   The vans are always coloured white, give or take a few logos, motifs, signs and crusted-on mud. This appears to be some type of special livery which marks out this breed of motorist, because without exception they all drive in the same way (see below).

(2)   The vans are always driven to the same appalling standards. Accelerators are floored, alternating with the brake pedals being floored; there are no half measures. This will explain why, no matter how fast you're driving your Volvo in your outside lane, all you can see in your rear view mirror is White Van Man's radiator badge. Should you be considerate enough to pull over he will scream past you regardless. However, with your clear duty to ensure that speed limits are obeyed you should refuse to move over. You will then find he will scream past you on the inside, scream *at* you on the way, and possibly accompany this with hand signals which are not normally found in the Standard Highway Code.

8.   FARM VEHICLES:

These used to be solely confined to fields where they were born to be used, only occasionally straying out onto the public highway to go from field to field. Nowadays, however, they appear to have the right to go anywhere they please and, much to the Volvo Driver's disgust and to the eternal discredit of the Highways Agency, now there's even special Highway Code signs condoning their use of the public highway.

Farm Vehicles generally come in two disguises; tractors and combine harvesters. Each has its own unique way of fouling up the roads:

8.1   Tractors - There is a little-known law passed way back in the mists of the last century which absolves tractors from conforming to any of the motoring laws and bye-laws that every other motorist has to observe, Volvos included. There can be no other explanation for these monstrosities lumbering around our roads with apparent impunity. Tractors are farm vehicles and that's where they should reasonably be expected to stay. Instead they take to the roads, usually where it's just too narrow to overtake, or sometimes even straight onto busy trunk roads.

They emerge from their farms and fields, wheels caked in mud and assorted substances too horrible to mention, straight onto the road in front of the Volvo Driver. The tractor driver would be more aware of you standing on your nose behind him, as you put the Volvo's ABS system through its paces, if he had a rear view mirror - but he hasn't got one. By now the road is a skidpan of muck and you, rightly incensed by his negligent behaviour, look for his licence plates to report him - but he doesn't have any of those, either. Having gathered speed to a brisk 15 mph the tractor now proceeds to bombard you with great clods of mud from his rear tyres as it chugs along. It is at this point that, as you rev up impatiently to get past him (while you can still actually see through your windscreen), your revving wheels encounter one of the clods of mud lying in wait on the road.

Your day is made complete when your Volvo is eventually pulled out of the ditch - by a tractor.

Note of Caution - beware of tractors pulling trailers. These can be a low-loader type piled high with bales of hay, or worse, a sinister miniature tanker covered in glob and a dripping valve. And you know, you just know, what's inside it. There's little point in winding up the tractor driver. He is totally impervious to constructive criticism and is prone to having an itchy trigger finger on the release valve of the miniature tanker of toxic waste that he's towing. Contact with this material will not enhance the re-sale value of your Volvo.

8.2   Combine Harvesters - The tractor's big brother. For blocking up a country road nothing acts faster than a combine harvester. And when I say blocking the road I mean *completely* blocking it - nothing can get past from either direction as it ambles along at jogging pace. Upon meeting one the Volvo Driver's only course of action is to perform an impromptu three-point turn and leg it away to seek an alternative route. This manoeuvre may temporarily inconvenience the motorists behind you but they will understand. In fact, if the truth be known, they will be impressed by your quick thinking and assertive actions.

9.   TRAMS:

Volvos are tough motors, built to minimise the chances of you coming off second best if some careless fool drives into you. This confidence contributes to the feelings of superiority when driving your Volvo. However, you have to know your limitations. There are still one or two types of road user you would be well advised not to take issue with and one of these is the tram. Trams are generally the lowest order of wheeled road users. They have no brain, and can only go in one pre-set direction (the direction in which the rails are pointing). Apart from designated tram stops and traffic lights they will stop for nothing else.

Trams are built like tanks and have therefore acquired a built-in immune system to other road users, so they make no distinction between a Volvo and any other road vehicle. Be warned. If you are silly enough to try your luck and a tram clobbers you it can irreversibly modify your Volvo and probably you with it.

After a judicious assessment of the risks involved it is highly recommended that the Volvo Driver should refuse to patronise towns that run trams and leave these silly citizens to play with their giant train set on their own. That'll show 'em.

10.   BUSES AND COACHES:

Some of the largest obstacles that the Volvo Driver has to contend with on his daily journeys are buses and coaches. There are many varieties and all of them are dedicated to making your journey as miserable as possible. As a Volvo Driver your over-riding objective is to get in front of the bus as soon as it is reasonably safe to do so without damaging your Volvo. It is at this point that the bus driver plays his trump card. Adding insult to injury you now find that one half of your road has been specially designated as a bus-only lane.

Now, bus lanes are for the exclusive use of buses, coaches and government ministers late for appointments, and draconian punishment awaits any humble motorist who snaps and decides to use them. Bus lanes are supposed to improve the efficiency of public transport, and this is fine if you happen to want to go exactly where the bus is going. If not, you will have to use your Volvo, along with the many thousand other commuting motorists who now find themselves stuck in interminable tailbacks caused through compacting what was once two lanes of free-flowing traffic into one lane of gridlock. However, as a Volvo Driver you are free from the shackles of conformity and you should regard the bus lane as your personal territory. After all, you have been set the perfect example and if it's good enough for politicians in their chauffeur-driven limos then it's certainly good enough for you - at least you pay the road tax to use it. There again, this could also explain why Volvo Drivers pick up more tickets for bus lane traffic violations than anybody else.

Here are some of the types of buses and coaches you will encounter on your travels, and the ploys they use to cause maximum grief and frustration to the Volvo Driver:

10.1   The Double-decker - Great big buses ambling around city centres, belching out fumes and stopping at bus stops every hundred yards on roads not quite wide enough for you to get by.

You sit impotently in your Volvo while the bus driver-cum-conductor painstakingly collects all the passengers' fares, and your demeanour is hardly improved when you read the sign on the back of the bus which says *"Please let the bus pull out"*. Like you have a choice.

10.2   The Bendy-bus - The latest innovation from continental Europe, based on an idea by Fisher Price. Double-deckers have one passenger deck on top of another. The Bendy-bus accommodates the same number of passengers but with one single-deck trailer attached to a single-deck bus by means of a giant rubber concertina. This makes the bus twice as long but allows it to go round bends and corners in two dimensions. This can be very disconcerting for the Volvo Driver who is not used to seeing long vehicles suddenly bend in the middle when going round bends and corners. This is bad enough, but the Bendy-bus also has other tricks up its sleeve to unsettle the Volvo Driver, such as:

- from the rear it gives the appearance of two single-deck buses travelling very close together. It's only when you start to overtake in a tight spot that you realise the two buses are joined at the hip and there is no gap to nip into.

- it moves with the speed of a constipated anaconda. It can't go any faster or it will "snake" all over the road, so getting stuck behind one can provide many opportunities for the Volvo Driver to practice his anger management.

- stopping at bus stops requires twice the kerb length of ordinary buses and since most bus stops haven't been built with this in mind the Bendy-bus just stops in the middle of the road. Or it parks the front end in the bus stop and leaves the back half sticking out, blocking the road anyway.

The Volvo Driver's best bet is to practice "bus avoidance"; i.e. buy a bus timetable and route map and work out ways of avoiding the bloody things altogether.

10.3   The City Hopper - Oversized Transit Vans with windows. They go where they want, when they want, and stop whenever the mood takes them. They are the loose cannons of public service vehicles and three or four of them together have been known to gridlock entire town centres.

10.4   The Express Coach -   Almost the size of double-decker buses, Express Coaches are designed for long-distance journeys on motorways. Their drivers look to long-distance lorry drivers (see next section) as their role models, and their favourite tricks include suddenly swerving into the fast lane in front of your Volvo, and maintaining a speed just 5 mph less than yours. When they eventually pull back into the inside lane they proceed to bomb downhill at speeds well in excess of the allowed limits. It is estimated that the safe stopping distance of one of these coaches, when fully laden with SAGA Holiday punters and their luggage, is measured in miles rather than feet. And that's on a dry road.

11.   TRUCKS, TANKERS, LORRIES, JUGGERNAUTS ETC....:

Unrivalled in their ability to make life a misery for the motorist. And, it pains me to admit, the Volvo Driver is no exception. Any motorist will come off second best in an argument with one of these brutes, due mainly to the fact that their drivers are cocooned twelve feet up in the air in their cabs with 40-odd tonnes of truck underneath and behind them to use as a weapon. They are quite capable of driving over a car without even realising it.
Lorries, or trucks as our US cousins call them, come in a variety of shapes and sizes, each one equipped to inflict their own unique brand of aggravation. They range from the humble dumper truck, through

furniture vans and oil tankers, to the 44-tonne juggernaut complete with identical trailer. The Standard Highway Code asks that you give way to the lorry to which, as a Volvo Driver, I offer a respectful "bollocks". When have you ever seen one give way to you? Precisely. It is widely suspected that a lorry driver undergoes secret special training and certainly most of them are meticulously skilled in the art of winding up the motorist, which they take to like a duck to water. So be prepared. The golden rule of the *Volvo Driver's Highway Code* is never, repeat **NEVER**, give way to the bastards, even when faced with the rare opportunity to be courteous to them. Don't give them an inch. They might be bigger than you, but you're faster and infinitely more manoeuvrable, and anyway they've got to catch you first.

Here are the main types of lorry and some of the pleasures that the Volvo Driver can look forward to, especially when they're travelling in the same direction. As before, see how many you can spot on a typical journey:

11.1   The Load Shedder - A typical variety is the builder's truck that takes to the road at 20 mph during rush hour loaded up with a vast pyramid of sand, gravel or chippings. In a desperate attempt to gain more speed these trucks will often lighten their load by gradually pouring it onto the road through the gap beneath the tailboard. As you're following it in a stream of traffic there's not much you can do by way of taking evasive action from the shower of flying gravel. However, since a lot of these lorries now have a little sign on the back that says *"Well driven? Telephone xxxxxxxxx"* at least you may have a contact number where you can send the bill for your respray. Well, it's worth a try.

A different variety involves a low-loader stacked precariously with pallets at a height just one inch short of all the bridges it's likely to go under. Quite often the low-loader builds up a head of speed and is sometimes required to negotiate a bend, which it does quite successfully. The pallets on the other hand go straight on. Should you find that

40

your Volvo is on the receiving end you would be strongly advised to look very seriously into the whole question of car insurance.

11.2   The Mobile Car Wash - Every motorists dream. 44-tonne artics doing 70 mph on a wet motorway. You need to get past, and you know you have the right to overtake, and therefore you should do so, regardless of visibility. Lock onto the rear lights of the vehicle in front and go for it. As you draw near the lorry it will shower you with spray and anything else it can chuck up all over your Volvo. Remember that it doesn't matter if visibility is zero because the rear lights of the vehicle in front are your "eyes". In your hurry to get past and keep the rear lights in front in your sights you are now doing 95 mph in dangerously slippery conditions. For a Volvo this is acceptable as you have supreme confidence in the car's road-holding, and you should stick by this principle when the spray clears to reveal that the vehicle in front also has blue lights on its roof to go with its red lights at the back.

11.3   The Duelling Lorries - These are specially reserved for 2-lane carriageways. The entire length of the A1 between London and Newcastle is favourite here. The system works something like this. Lorry No 2 sits behind Lorry No 1 on the inside lane; speed of both approximately 40 mph. Your Volvo is in its rightful place on the outside lane at a law-abiding 70 mph, and of course you are late having just successfully negotiated a Load Shedder (see 11.1) and a Mobile Car Wash (see 11.2). As you approach Lorry No 2 it suddenly veers across in front of you into the outside lane to overtake Lorry No 1. He then signals to indicate that he has done so. This causes you to brake sharply and to wonder aloud whether the mother of the driver ever knew what his father's last name was. But Lorry No 2 is fully loaded and of course there is now an incline. So Lorry No 2 sits on the outside lane doing 41 mph alongside Lorry No 1 who is maintaining 40 mph, After three or four miles, having built up a nice five-mile tailback, Lorry No 2 eventually gets past Lorry No 1 and swings back into the inside lane in front of Lorry No 1. This is accompanied by a mysterious sequence of left and right flashers from both lorries which is obviously a code known only to themselves.

Free to overtake at last you must get past quick-smart before Lorry No 1 decides its time for his piece of the action and tries to overtake Lorry No 2. Believe me, it happens. Once past the lorries you must register your disapproval with this affront to the Volvo. Having overtaken the two lorries swing into the inside lane just in front of Lorry No 2. For added effect try and make sure you're going uphill at the time. Then, ***without*** hitting your brakes, (the brake lights will alert him) slow down imperceptibly using the gearbox or just use the natural loss of momentum from going uphill. The driver of Lorry No 2 will wonder what the hell you're doing as you loom up in front of him. Now slow down to about 20 mph for a few seconds. This will cause him to lose the head of steam he's built up over the last few miles and, amidst much effing and blinding, frantically work his way down the gearbox from sixth to first, almost stopping in order to get his momentum going again. This will take him several minutes and will be a salutary lesson to him. See how he likes it. Then speed off in your Volvo in a glow of self-righteous satisfaction, over the brow of the next hill - straight into two lines of stationary traffic trying to negotiate a new set of road works on the carriageway.

11.4   The Siamese Twins - Two container lorries from the same company hit the road together. And stay together. Presumably because they can't bear the thought of being parted. So they rumble along the road nose-to-tail, just inches apart, making it well-nigh impossible for anybody to overtake. Any ordinary motorist, that is - they've reckoned without the Volvo Driver. Safe in the knowledge that the truck drivers will show due deference and ease back to let you slip in between them during overtaking, you go for it. Then they close the gap, leaving you up an inlet without a paddle. The best course of action then is retreat, knowing that the rest of the cars behind the trucks will make way for you. When you do eventually overtake convey your sentiments through the sunroof *(see section 17.9)* using appropriate sign language and hand signals - just as you shoot past the jam sandwich parked up on the side which you couldn't see before because of the length of the two trucks.

11.5   The Long Vehicle - It says "Long Vehicle" on the back but you're never quite sure how long it actually is. This only becomes apparent once you start to overtake. Once past the point of no-return you discover that it is, in fact, carrying a large girder, the sort that supports King's Cross station, and the entire truck is twice as long as "normal" long vehicles. This is the sort of challenge the Volvo Driver relishes and it becomes a supreme test of skill and judgement to floor it and safely get through the gap between the truck and the on-coming traffic. You will, of course, make it - just - and the expense involved in replacing your wing mirrors can be considered a small price to pay for the privilege of being able to demonstrate your driving skills.

11.6   The Car Transporter -   a Classic Tale of Evolution - Once upon a time a team of boffins was asked to design a method of delivering new cars to showrooms without actually driving them there. So the idea of carting them around on a specially designed truck was born. This became known as the *Car Transporter*. Now this Car Transporter was designed to hold four cars as two layers of two cars on an articulated trailer and was considered to be a pioneering breakthrough at the time. As technology developed this quietly became six cars as two layers of three. Then the backroom boys responsible for designing these monstrosities really began to get adventurous and added an extra layer, allowing **nine** cars to be transported instead of six. Then they bust a fuse and set themselves the task of trying to cram on as many cars as possible to "maximise efficiency". They couldn't add any more layers because the first bridge it went under would have knocked the whole contraption back to three layers again. So they set about cunningly altering the angles the cars were fixed at on the ramps, "dovetailing" more and more cars into the same amount of space. Then madness took hold and they added a second trailer with the same loading capacity.

Now, all this has progressed without any regard to the damage being done to the road surfaces and other environmental issues such as the huge fume-belching obstacles they present to the Volvo Driver. They also tend to play at being Siamese Twins *(see section 11.4)* when there is more than one of them. Nor do they crawl along. They speed excessively for the load they're carrying and occasionally have been known to pay the price when one of them loses control and rolls over on the motorway to have its tummy tickled, scattering its load of shiny new cars all over the place. For the Volvo Driver who witnesses such a calamity this can be a very traumatic experience, for two reasons:

- he will get held up in a 20-mile tailback while the wrecked cars and transporter are cleared away;

- (even more traumatising) - he discovers that those shiny new cars being transported are Volvos.

12.   ABNORMAL LOADS:

The ultimate mobile road blocks; huge low-loaders weighted down with an assortment of artefacts which most sane people wouldn't dream of bringing onto the roads. Getting stuck behind one offers the Volvo Driver a journey of untold misery. The first hint that you have of an abnormal load being driven up the motorway in front of you is when you join a 15-mile tailback. An hour or so later distant flashing amber lights confirm your worst fears as you spot the load plodding along on the horizon.

Abnormal loads almost always exhibit three characteristics:

(1)   Their average speed is 10 mph, and that's downhill on a good day. Uphill, and the Volvo Driver would make much better progress if he parked up and walked the rest of the way down the hard shoulder.

(2)   They will effectively use up two lanes of the motorway. Not so bad if it's a three-lane motorway; very bad if it's a two-lane motorway.

(3)   They will be accompanied by one, possibly two, jam sandwiches with full flashing red and blue lights, and maybe the odd motorcycle out-rider. Now you may think that this would mean two or three police vehicles out of circulation from normal traffic duties. You would be wrong. The long arm of the law is quite capable of buzzing ahead on his radio to a mobile Mr Plod with more time on his hands to nab the odd Volvo Driver who has been tempted to take liberties.

All this, of course, assumes that the abnormal load *is* on a motorway. In such cases the only conceivable way around it is to leave the motorway at the first available exit, leg it along the parallel A-class roads, and re-join the motorway a bit further up in front of the monster. The only drawback here is when two-thirds of the motorway decide to do exactly the same thing and you find yourself gridlocked on a back road and in a more untenable position than you were before. Of course, should the abnormal load be on a single carriageway road, forget it. Go home.

So, what are these abnormal loads? Let's take a look at the main varieties that you're likely to encounter on one of your more frustrating journeys in your Volvo:

12.1   The Apartment Block - Great half-built timber-framed houses, or mobile homes. These are centred on enormous trailers with several feet of overhang on each side to provide that extra adrenaline rush when overtaking.

12.2   The Starlight Express - Railway carriages, and even steam locomotives from the golden age of rail travel, have often been seen being transported on low-loaders from one end of the country to the other. Presumably, actually moving them on the railway tracks provided for that purpose is too easy.

12.3   The Intergalactic Moon Buggy - Huge 4-wheeled dumper trucks for driving around earthworks and the larger construction sites. Given the speed at which these low-loaders move better progress would be made if they scrapped the low-loader altogether and just drove the Intergalactic Moon Buggy on the motorway as it is. The downside of this is that the Moon Buggy could drive over vehicles, Volvos included, in complete and blissful ignorance.

12.4   The Mutated Cotton Reel - Giant cable drums lashed down onto a low-loader and trailed around the country. These often travel as Siamese Twins *(see section 11.4)*, complete with multiple police out-riders that effectively prevent any overtaking, adding that extra dimension of grief for the Volvo Driver trapped in the tailback.

12.5   Tanks 'n' Things - To practice defending the realm the armed forces are occasionally mobilised for "manoeuvres". This means moving their trucks and armoured cars around the country by road. Your road. To complete the set they bring their tanks with them too, piggy-backing them onto low-loaders just like the Intergalactic Moon Buggy (above). Also like the Moon Buggy, they would make better progress if they dispensed with the low-loader and drove the tanks straight onto the road. If nothing else it would wipe the smiles off the faces of the Company Rep and Boy Racer, to say nothing of the fun they could have with drivers of the fairer sex. But the Volvo Driver is different class and would not be intimidated by the presence of a tank on the public highway. After all, take out the tank's gun turret, replace the caterpillar tracks with wheels and put in a few windows and what have you got? A Volvo. The Volvo and the tank; not so much blood brothers as diesel brothers. Forged from the same stock. We rest our case.

12.6   The Caterpillar Monster - Never mind the tank; there is an even bigger monster at large wearing caterpillar tracks instead of wheels. This is the bulldozer, and is so large and unwieldy that when it sits on a low-loader the caterpillars actually hang over the edge while the low-loader itself buckles precariously under its weight. With or without motorcycle outriders it does add that extra thrill of uncertainty when you do eventually get the chance to overtake.

13.   VEHICLES BELONGING TO THE LOCAL COUNCIL:

The Mission Statement of all local councils is built around their commitment to inflict as much misery as possible on the motorist. Their ability to wreck any smooth-flowing traffic system with speed humps, one-way streets, pedestrianisation schemes, bus / cycle lanes and a host of other fiendishly contrived obstacles (see later) is unrivalled. If this wasn't bad enough they also have a fleet of their own special vehicles which they let loose to wander aimlessly around the roads to block up the traffic. So, let's see what the councils have lying in wait for the unsuspecting Volvo Driver:

13.1   Refuse Collection Vehicles *(politically correct)* / **Waste Management Vehicles** *(politically correct)* / **Dustcarts** *(politically incorrect)* - Fortunately, these usually emerge once a week, but they will infest different parts of the town on different days of the week. Gone are the old-fashioned dustcarts. Today's model is large, slow, noisy and equipped with a giant munching machine for compacting the trash. They're also not fussy about where they park.

To avoid the rush-hour grid-locks on the main roads you will be using the rat-runs as you whizz round the back streets in your Volvo, slowing down only for the occasional speed hump. A cocktail of learner drivers, cyclists, lollipop persons and thoughtlessly-parked cars have combined to make you late and the rat-run offers an opportunity to make up some time. Then you whip round the corner into another side street and there, smack in the middle of the road, is a refuse collection truck doing its stuff. You will now need to park up and wander over to the driver to ask him to move the truck to let you through. Explain that you have a busy day ahead and that you're late for an important strategy meeting. He will be impressed. Tell him that, unlike him, you have a proper job to do. He will be even more impressed. It is at this point that you realise you should have parked a bit further away as you wonder just how long it's going to take you to dig your Volvo out from underneath a dozen dustbins' worth of rotting vegetation, used cat litter, old baked bean cans and sundry other domestic waste products.

13.2   Gritting Lorries - These are the trucks the council use for gritting icy roads and are very similar to the Load Shedder *(see section 11.1)*, except that the council gritting lorry is designed to ***deliberately*** shed its load all over the motorway. They are quite rare specimens, these gritting lorries. Rumour has it that this is because they are expensive vehicles so the council can only afford one or two, having spent most of its budget on painting cycle lanes, installing speed cameras, building all manner of traffic calming measures, and financing cowboy wheel-clamping contractors. Then there is the cost of all the salt and grit, and this isn't cheap, oh dear me, no. So the gritting lorries must be used sparingly and brought out only when it is considered they will be most effective. This usually follows lengthy council-chamber debates on the subject, by which time the temperature has risen above freezing and it's pouring with rain, so washing away all that expensive salt and grit. As soon as the roads freeze over, or it starts to snow, the gritting lorries stay under cover. Too cold, you see.

Fortunately, the Volvo Driver has no real need of gritting lorries since his Volvo Awareness Training will have taught him how to cope with ice and snow *(see section 20.2)*. So on the rare occasions that you do find yourself stuck behind one you will realise that there is absolutely no need to stay there and have your entire car covered with salt and your beautiful paintwork shot-blasted with grit. You will need to get past it quick-smart, and of course when you do you will drive straight onto that part of the road that hasn't been gritted yet and is still covered with ice. Your next challenge will be getting your Volvo out of the old lady's front garden, ignoring the hand signals from the driver of the grit lorry as it chugs past, whilst maintaining an air of nonchalant superiority. Difficult, but not impossible, for the Volvo Driver.

13.3   Grass Cutters - Council grass cutters are usually of two types. Either a miniature tractor or what looks like a dumbed-down quad bike, both of which will be towing a mower and armed with a flashing amber light on a pole. They are used to cut the grass in municipal parks and on roadside verges. The problem with this is that these grass cutters are required to reach these parks and verges under their own steam, and they're generally not too worried about how they get there. They make no distinction between Volvos, other vehicles, and even pedestrians, all of which are ignored in their relentless quest to reach their grass-cutting destinations. From the Volvo Driver's point of view he would do well to take on board a few facts concerning the grass cutter to prepare him for the challenges that lie in wait around our urban green belts:

- Grass cutters never venture out alone. It is quite common for them to travel in convoys of three or four as they race around the roads.

- They are infinitely adaptable to a wide range of surfaces. As well as grass they can be seen successfully traversing roads, pavements, private driveways, cycle lanes and bus lanes. In fact, anything goes.

- They are colour-blind, and hence cannot deal with traffic lights. To avoid this they mount the pavements at junctions and whizz round behind the traffic lights - just like a cyclist, in fact.

13.4   Road Sweepers & Drain Cleaners - The mechanical kind, not a horny-handed son of toil armed with a broom. For the benefit of the Volvo Driver, mechanical road sweepers can be characterised by the following features:

● They are ponderous and woefully slow. 2 mph is favourite, as they align themselves with the gutters and proceed to sweep most of the rubbish around with rotating metal brushes. Some of it even gets swept up. There is a strong temptation to treat them as parked, except that they keep moving, which tends to upset the Volvo Driver's battle plans.

● They are usually left-hand drive. This is not necessarily because they are part of a job lot from Albania (though they could be) but so that the drivers can lean out of their nearside windows to inspect the efficiency of the gutter sweeping process.

● They make a hell of a noise. This can be an advantage if you've left your Volvo parked on the road. If you hear one approaching get out and move the Volvo pronto before the road sweeper works its way round your car, taking the walls out of your offside tyres with its rotating brushes in the process.

● Some are tankers equipped with a large hose for cleaning drains. Like enormous mechanical ant-eaters they dunk their hoses into roadside drains and other repositories of effluent and suck up the contents to be transported away and dumped in much larger repositories of effluent. This will eventually become the foundation of a building site for a development of prestigious luxury homes.

Note of Caution: It would be unwise for the Volvo Driver, in this instance, to take issue with the driver of one of these vehicles on matters of blocking up the public highway with their filthy tankers, and similar sensitive subjects. We will leave it to the Volvo Driver's imagination if the tanker driver decides to point the hose at his Volvo and switch to "blow" instead of "suck".

14.   VEHICLES BELONGING TO CONSTRUCTION SITES:

In the same way as Farm Vehicles *(see section 8)* often escape from their native agricultural habitat to jam up the traffic on the Volvo Driver's roads, so do vehicles working on building / construction sites. Now construction sites are home to many types of vehicle; at any one time you may be able to spot skip lorries, cement lorries, dumper trucks, mobile cranes, Intergalactic Moon Buggies and the humble JCB. Lorries and Moon Buggies we have covered in previous sections; it's the mobile crane and the JCB that concern us here. On-site they have an essential part to play, but unfortunately they don't stay there. More often than not they get the urge to wander onto the roads and the Volvo Driver is faced with yet more aggro as he attempts to travel from A to B unmolested. Let's look at them both:

14.1   Mobile Cranes - As for abnormal loads *(see section 12)* these are usually found at the front of a 6-mile tailback on a busy trunk road, or turning a three-lane motorway into a two-lane motorway as they lumber up the inside lane, effectively blocking it off for any traffic wanting to travel faster than 25 mph. Mobile cranes usually have eight big wheels and a huge jib lying flat on the roof with a six foot overhang over the driver's cab. It's really quite pointless for the Volvo Driver to try and take issue with a mobile crane. For a start, to do so would be to acknowledge that the crane actually has a right to be on the road, which we all know is not the case. Far better just to ignore it. If you do feel the urge to wave at the crane's driver make sure you've got safely past it first, and out of range of the jib.

14.2   JCBs - One of the most despised vehicles on the roads. And the bottom line is that JCBs shouldn't even be *on* the roads because, like their little brother the tractor, JCBs were born to work off-road on construction sites. But in order to get from site to site they use the road. Your road; the Volvo Driver's road, and with little concern over *how* they use it. They are also totally immune from the laws and requirements of the Standard Highway Code, and remain oblivious to all other road users as they charge along at a breakneck 25 mph, with their great buckets bouncing up and down.

JCBs are responsible for some of the worst traffic gridlocks on the roads. Many is the time a JCB has been spotted in town centres, practising their 0-to-20-mph-in-five-minutes-from-a-standing-start at traffic lights, and performing the JCB version of a handbrake turn around roundabouts. Unfortunately, this is yet another example of the Volvo Driver being unable to do anything meaningful to combat this menace. You could try the slowing-down techniques used on the Duelling Lorries *(see section 11.3)*, or the spoof brakelight effects normally reserved for caravans *(section 6)*, but you will need to ensure beforehand that the traffic conditions will permit a quick getaway. Failure to do so may result in your Volvo having an unscheduled stay in a Volvo body repair shop while the big bucket-shaped dents are hammered out of your roof.

15.   THE WORLD'S SLOWEST VEHICLES:

These are ponderous vehicle oddities that we can't classify anywhere else in this book. They are *always* very slow-moving and therefore offer even more opportunities to throw a spanner in the works of the Volvo Driver's travel plans. They are the scourge of the highways, and four main types have been identified:

15.1   Electric Vehicles - In a pioneering step to try and reduce environmental pollution these vehicles don't have conventional engines. Instead they are powered by great big electric batteries which are put on charge every night; much like your mobile phone, in fact.

It is also an irrefutable principle of science that a vehicle powered by batteries isn't likely to give a T5 a run for its money in terms of performance; in fact its top speed struggles to get into double figures. They are therefore pretty efficient at causing obstructions and jam-ups in town centres, their usual habitat, and where the Volvo Driver is as likely as anybody else to get snarled up in the traffic.

Electric vehicles are generally of two types:

1.   *Milk Floats* - fortunately these are usually only encountered in the small hours when there's not much traffic about. Just as well, really, as they are often seen at the end of their shift crawling back to their depots for the long-overdue appointment with the electrical mains.

2.   *Powered Vehicles used by Disabled People* - these have been likened to electric shopping trolleys with seats. With a top speed of 8 mph they can be seen gliding noiselessly along the road, sometimes even the pavements, without a care in the world. The Volvo Driver should, however, be on his guard since the more elderly the driver the more unpredictable they are. Listed below are some of the more original manoeuvres practised by elderly drivers of electric vehicles, and the Volvo Driver would do well to remain vigilant at all times:

•   The sudden decision to want to be on the other side of the road. No signals, no waiting for proper zebra or pelican crossings - just veering across the road regardless.

•   Once across the road they cut across cycle lanes and bus lanes, mount the pavement and drive straight into Tesco's.

- Taking a wrong turning and bombing down a slip road onto a dual carriageway or, God forbid, a motorway.

- Ditto, but going the wrong way up a motorway.

Research has indicated that it is performing tricks like these that probably qualified the driver for a disabled person's vehicle in the first place.

15.2   Hearses and Funeral Processions - You thought it was bad enough when assorted nimrods such as the Sunday Driver, Boy Racer, cyclists and motorcyclists ganged up on you to frustrate you during your journey. To your great concern you now find that they can louse things up for you from beyond the grave. They do this when making their final journey to the cemetery or crematorium and where, for reasons that escape us, it is deemed necessary to travel at the speed of a slug in a bag. Being the thoughtful and unselfish breed that they are many Volvo Drivers have gone on record as saying that once they shuffle off this mortal coil they would not wish to be the cause of a traffic jam and their funeral cortege should travel at normal Volvo speeds. Unfortunately, to their great discredit the authorities have yet to accept this point of view. The official party line is that this would be disrespectful, whereas in reality it is widely suspected that it would be terminally embarrassing should a fully-laden hearse be nicked for speeding.

15.3   Steamrollers - These days they're not steam-driven but even so they are not to be argued with at any cost. And when you think about it there's really no need to. Steamrollers are so slow as to be almost stationary, so the Volvo Driver can quite easily treat one as being parked. Be careful though; they're not called steamrollers for nothing. Do not, under any circumstances, attempt any trials of strength, or dispute any rights of way, with a steamroller. If you do, you may well find that your Volvo will take on an entirely different shape. In extreme cases you may take on an entirely different shape as well which will do absolutely nothing for your campaign to establish the Volvo Driver as the King of the Road.

15.4   Elderly Drivers - These are drivers who are long past retirement age yet stubbornly cling to the belief that they're just as good a driver today as they were in 1948. And they won't hear a word to the contrary. In reality, however, they are nothing but a bloody nuisance to all and sundry. At a time when most of their contemporaries are hanging up their car keys and entering retirement homes these mobile coffin-dodgers make it their mission in life to keep driving for as long as possible. Nothing discourages them, certainly not little issues such as being half-blind or having the attention span of a goldfish. Just what the Volvo Driver needs. Elderly Drivers exhibit some unmistakeable characteristics:

- Elderly male drivers always wear flat caps. Elderly female drivers have a frizz of thinning grey hair and appear to be no more than three feet tall as they peer through the steering wheel. Both wear glasses.

- They cannot, or will not, exceed 40 mph. This probably dates back to the days when a car's top speed *was* 40 mph.

- Modern in-car technology such as indicators, windscreen washers, heated rear windows and 5-speed gearboxes remain a complete mystery to them. In fact many Elderly Drivers are struggling to cope with the passing of the starting handle.

- They always know best, as characterised by their determination to dictate the speed of traffic trapped behind them as they cruise along at 35 mph in the outside lane of a dual carriageway.

- They have formed a deep and meaningful relationship with their cars, much like the Sunday Driver. The type of car that the Elderly Driver owns is usually one of two types:

(1)   A small Ford / Honda / Nissan family saloon which he bought new in 1978 and has kept ever since. Total mileage on the clock does not exceed 30,000 miles and it will have rarely, if ever, been driven over 50 mph.

(2)   A top-of-the-range Merc, BMW or even a Volvo which he's saved up for all his life and now he's got it he's too old to drive it properly.

The Elderly Driver just about realises what other road users actually are, so it is safe to assume that he won't be aware of the implications of holding up a Volvo Driver as a result of his thoughtless driving. In terms of action there's really not a lot you can do apart from campaigning for all drivers over the age of 65 to be compulsorily re-tested. This could, of course, backfire on the Volvo Driver when *he* reaches 65 but as we know there are always allowances for special cases.

16.   FOREIGN DRIVERS:

There is one final category of road user that the Volvo Driver has to consider, and that is the driver that visits these shores from foreign parts. Once upon a time the number of Foreign Drivers coming here was limited by virtue of the fact that we're surrounded by water. The restricting factor was the small number of car ferry services that operated to and from continental Europe. Once the UK became fully integrated into the European Union passage between member states technically became easier, and a few more ferry and then hovercraft services started up. Even then we were able to cope with the increasing influx of four-wheeled tourists. And then they opened the Channel Tunnel. Then the EU expanded, taking in many of the old Eastern Bloc countries and widening the scope of nationalities taking to our roads. This was followed by new long-distance ferry services from Scandinavia, Holland and Germany and within a relatively short space of time the Volvo Driver's roads were being over-run. This was taking place at the same time as our own domestic traffic increased, putting an even greater strain on our road network.

Now, the Volvo Driver faces enough challenges on a daily basis from our own road users without Johnny Foreigner invading us to add to the turmoil. Our continental friends bring with them their own unique brands of aggression to inflict on the Volvo Driver. For example, in their native habitat most of them drive on the wrong side of the road; their vehicles are left hand drive so they can't see properly to overtake or change lanes when they get here; they can't speak our language to ask for directions. And there are increasing numbers of them because our immigration officials seem to have little control over who they let in to terrorise us. Immediate examples that spring to mind are the huge juggernauts and trailers that hammer the hell out of our roads, and the reclaimed insurance write-offs that seem to find their way here from East German scrapyards. Then there are the continental standards of driving which in general are appalling. Truly, the Volvo Driver faces a multitude of challenges.

Then, if this wasn't bad enough we now have those that arrive by plane from the other side of the world and take to our roads in rental cars. This is even more frightening since UK rental cars have UK licence plates and so you don't even know they're here.

So who are these Foreign Drivers and why do they come here? After all, we have the highest fuel costs and road taxes in the civilised western world, and one of the worst maintained and congested road networks in Europe. We also have high consumer prices and bloody awful weather. So what's the big attraction? Let's look at some of the nationalities that you will find driving around the Volvo Driver's roads, and you may gain a better appreciation of what to expect when you encounter one of our foreign friends. So let's welcome them, Eurovision-style. ***Come on down!!.....***

16.1 Sven & Ingrid from Sweden - These are nice friendly people with an excellent taste in cars; i.e. they will probably be driving a Volvo. So they should be since Sweden is, after all, Volvoland. Just like their country they will plod along at a sedate pace. They will have a Volvo full of little Svens and Ingrids and their main purpose of visiting us is the *Great MetroCentre Day Trip*. This is a bit like the Great British Booze Cruise in reverse; with the new overnight ferries from Scandinavia we are becoming hosts to hordes of Viking families anxious to spend their euros on all things British. Back they go, loaded up with Marmite, Pot Noodles and the latest Marks & Sparks fashion range. Sad as they are, they should nevertheless be welcomed by our Volvo Drivers.

16.2 Hans & Helga from Germany - If you think you've got problems with all the other road users you ain't seen nuthin' until you cop a German family fresh off the ferry. They drive the same way as they do in the Fatherland and remember that, at the time of writing this book, Germany is the only country left in Europe that has no speed limits on its autobahns. It can therefore take Hans a little while to adjust to our more sedate driving, but the Volvo Driver must make absolutely *no* allowances for this. When in Rome, and all that. So when you meet up with Hans and Helga you will need to subject them to the full repertoire of the Volvo Driver's tricks and manoeuvres to remind them of their position in the pecking order of the motoring world. They may not like it, and may even offer gestures of disapproval but, hey, who won the bloody war, anyway?

16.3 Luigi & Lucia from Italy - The Italian Highway Code definitely seems to be different from our Standard Highway Code. For example, most Italian drivers think that there's only two pedals in a manual car - the accelerator and the brake. Italian women are discouraged from driving, so it's Luigi who takes the wheel. Much like White Van Man over here *(see section 7)* Luigi's driving technique is to flatten the accelerator and the brake in alternate movements. Also, just like White Van Man, he will totally lose it if you so much as attempt to impede his progress on the roads. In fact rumour has it that, back in Italy, driving on the autostradas (Italian motorways) has replaced the chariot tracks in the amphitheatres as entertainment. The trouble with all this is that Luigi needs to learn that he can't import his driving methods to these shores. Fortunately, previous experiences with White Van Man will have hardened the Volvo Driver as to what to expect if an Italian licence plate is spotted, and he can plan accordingly.

16.4   Pierre & Fifi from France - The French drive a bit like the Italians but they're not quite so careful or considerate. Pierre and Fifi are the perfect French couple, just visiting us for a short break. Of course, they don't *like* us but it's the only place in Europe where they can get a decent cup of tea and curry sauce with their chips. As the archetypal French couple they are perfectly balanced - they have a chip (not a French fry) on both shoulders; one because they don't like the English, and the other because they don't like Volvos. And they don't like Volvos because they are better cars than French cars, so you can imagine their opinion of an English Volvo Driver. Do we care? No. When they come here they have to like it or lump it, which is something the French don't find easy to accept. So the Volvo Driver should do his bit towards *entente cordiale* and extend a typical Volvo Driver's welcome. This can be achieved by judicious use of the horn, flashing headlights and some of the greeting signals you will find in section 25 of this book, which can be interpreted in any language.

16.5   Carlos & Consuela from Spain - The Spanish don't have a Highway Code, at least not one that we're aware of, which goes a long way towards explaining the way they drive. Anything goes; driving on the left or the right, triple parking, sometimes stopping for red lights and sometimes not. This is probably why you never see many Volvos in Spain, since no self-respecting Volvo Driver would want to drive there. However, this does not prevent our typical Spanish couple Carlos and Consuela from visiting the English Volvo Driver on his own patch, which they occasionally do. Fortunately you don't find that many since the Spanish tend to favour the sunnier climates, but if you do come across one you will need to exercise a degree of caution. There are certain tell-tale signs which can identify our continental couple as Spanish. The first give-away is the "E" nationality plate on the back of the car. No, the car doesn't come from Estonia; it comes from Spain (España). The next clues are the dents and scratches on the car's bodywork, caused through normal Spanish driving conditions. The final clue will be the driving techniques - cruising along the outside lane of an empty motorway, parking up on double yellow lines, ignoring Lollipop Persons, etc - in other words tactics straight out of the *Volvo Driver's Highway Code*. Now, the Volvo Driver doesn't like being played at his own game on his own territory, and especially by a left-hand drive sardine can with a funny licence plate that has no business here in the first place. You will therefore need to welcome Carlos and Consuela with some of the tricks outlined in this book, but be careful. The dents and scratches on their car are battle scars, and the re-sale value of their car is probably zilch, so they won't be afraid to mix it. Whether or not they choose to take on a Volvo is another matter, but do you really want to chance it? Best to give them a wide berth and let some other mug take up the challenge.

16.6   Willi & Wilhemina from Belgium - Where? Belgium. The most boring country on God's green earth. France used to mostly border Holland in the north but France's northern regions were so flat, damp and miserable nobody really wanted to live there. Holland's southern regions were also flat, damp and miserable and nobody wanted to live there either. So a hundred or so years ago some genius hit on the idea of taking the northern bit of France and the southern bit of Holland and turning it into one flat, damp and miserable independent state. They called it Belgium. These days it's pretty cosmopolitan, what with it being at the centre of the European gravy train, but you rarely see any actual Belgians. This is because they're all too embarrassed to admit that they live there and to avoid actually having to be in Belgium more than they need to most Belgians spend their time travelling on the roads in and around Europe. Our Belgian couple, Willi and Wilhemina are no exception. Willi and Wilhemina travel here courtesy of the ferries from Ostend and Zeebrugge and can be easily identified by two things:

- Their car has a "B" nationality plate, and the licence plates are white and red with of course the circle of little yellow stars on a blue background to signify their allegiance to the European Superstate. Well, they've got nothing else to cling on to.

- Their bloody awful driving. The inner ring road in Brussels is a nightmare, with the average speed of vehicles about 80 mph. Willi and Wilhemina will have been weaned on this so when they get here they drive the same way. It's instinct. This presents another headache for the Volvo Driver and as before it's best to avoid and ignore them wherever possible.

16.7   Johann & Ludwig from Switzerland - From the land of cuckoo clocks, army knives, cheese with holes in and trains that run on time we welcome Johann and Ludwig, our alternative European couple. The Swiss are the genetic opposites of the Spanish and Italians. The latter do things as and when they feel like it, if at all, and can act up all extravagant and emotional. The Swiss, on the other hand, are very calm, organised, thorough and precise. Of all the Foreign Drivers on our roads Johann and Ludwig will be the ones driving at the correct speed limit and obeying every last dot and comma of our motoring laws. Quite right, too. Unless, as a Volvo Driver, you're stuck behind them on a winding country road. They are then immediately put into the same category as the Sunday Driver or Learner Driver and should be shown the same degree of tolerance, i.e. zero. However, being Swiss, Johann and Ludwig will not be fazed one iota by any inducement to drive faster and a bit of motorway aggro isn't going to bother them. Nor will they be intimidated by a Volvo Driver. After all, they've seen the bigger picture. As a nation they resolutely refuse to join the EU despite being landlocked by EU States. It has been suggested that their air of nonchalant superiority could possibly have something to do with them having the EU leaders by the *cojones* since all their slush funds are stashed away in numbered Swiss accounts. Who knows? Who cares.

16.8   Dai & Blodwyn from Wales - Yes, Wales. And it is a foreign country because FIFA says so. The Welsh were very quick to jump on the bandwagon when Mr Blair sold them the idea of devolution. The trouble is, it didn't go far enough. If the English had been properly consulted on the matter Offa's Dyke would have become a physical international border from the Severn to the Dee, complete with razor wire, sentry posts, gun turrets and a no-man's land between fences patrolled by nasty dogs. In fact it has been suggested that the only good things to come out of Wales are the roads to England.

Like the French, the Welsh don't like us very much, but they can't do without us because most of the funding for their Toytown Welsh Assembly still comes out of the pockets of the English taxpayer. So they feel obliged to visit us, usually by road, which means invading the English Volvo Driver's territory. Dai and Blodwyn are our typical Welsh couple. They arrive here unchallenged through the lack of border controls and as their car licence plates are the same format as ours you won't even know they're here. But they know they've arrived. After the valleys, England seems like Eldorado but once here they don't actually travel very far. This may be due to the fact that, once in England, those appalling bilingual Welsh / English road signs give way to signs in just plain English and they're lost. Dai and Blodwyn even have their own "language" which nobody outside Wales speaks, or wants to speak, so they feel a bit intimidated when faced with English-speaking people. The Volvo Driver should therefore be able to spot Dai and Blodwyn quite easily. They're usually within 30 miles of the border wandering around looking out of place. No need to worry. If you meet them the kindest thing to do is to put them out of our misery and point them back in the direction of the Severn Bridges. It is not wise to engage them in conversation. If they lapse into Welsh you'll spend the next twenty minutes combing the phlegm out of your hair.

16.9   Seamus & Colleen from Ireland - From the pretty Emerald Isle we greet our Irish couple, Seamus and Colleen. Now Seamus and Colleen are from the Republic of Ireland and their distinctive licence plates are a dead give-away to the Volvo Driver. Unfortunately their chronic driving is also a dead give-away to the Volvo Driver who would do well to stay on his guard. The Irish drive at one of two extremes, with no half measures. They either crawl along at 25 mph or race around at 90 mph, which, considering the state of most of the roads in their native country, enables them to live life on the edge, so to speak. But these lovely people are not the sharpest knives in the drawer. Without knowing any better Seamus and Colleen import their driving skills here and end up being a danger to themselves and everybody else they come into contact with - sometimes literally.

Our road signs also offer them a challenge. For example, they think that "KEEP RIGHT" is a political instruction, and when they see "KEEP LEFT" a few miles further on they get all confused. To them a "P" sign indicates roadside toilet facilities and Seamus's interpretation of "HUMPS FOR 500 METRES" doesn't bear thinking about.

16.10   Kostas & Cleo from Greece - Greek drivers. Now there's a contradiction in terms. You can either be Greek or be able to drive a car, but you can't be both. Trouble is, Kostas thinks he can. He spends his days chugging up and down hillsides and racing along the cart-tracks that pass for roads in Greece in his clapped-out banger, belching out black exhaust and scaring chickens. He knows what to press to make his car stop and go but his knowledge of the finer points of driving is zero. All of which makes him a total liability when he and his partner Cleo land here, pick up a rental car and take to the roads. Should Kostas and Cleo have ambitions for a longer stay in this country, for example to work in a Greek restaurant or in our vibrant black economy, then he is more likely to purchase his car. This won't cost him more than £50 and he finds a wide selection of suitable vehicles available to him at the many scrapyards around the country. Being ever-careful with money he saves on such trivialities as road tax, insurance, MOT testing and servicing, preferring to think of his vehicle as disposable.

It is when the Volvo Driver is having a really bad day, thinking that things could not get much worse, that he encounters Kostas and Cleo veering towards him as they struggle to get their car's steering to work. Once again, the Volvo Driver is forced into a split-second decision regarding rights of way and the action to be taken. Under the circumstances diving for cover might seem like a good idea.

16.11 Hank & Martha from the USA - I must confess to a love of all things American. The country, the people, the quality of life and the friendliness. Everything, in fact, except their drivers. American drivers are, without a shadow of a doubt, the wackiest in the western world and they are typified by our American couple, Hank and Martha. Now Hank is from Texas, a big State with lots of wide open spaces. His wife Martha, also from Texas, is a big lady with lots of wide open mouth. He drives; she back-seat drives.

Hank's driving techniques, to coin a crude American expression, suck, but he doesn't know any better so when they arrive in the UK and pick up their rental car from the airport they bring their driving madness with them. The Volvo Driver must therefore be on his guard at all times especially as there really isn't any obvious way to tell whether a car is rented, or what nationality the driver is. There are, however, a few tell-tale signs that unmistakeably identify our couple as American. For example:

●   Unless they've been here before they won't know what a roundabout is because they don't have them in the US. So having been programmed to drive on the right when they encounter a roundabout they go round them in the wrong direction, with predictably disastrous results.

- They cannot handle speed. American cars might be big but generally they're gutless. Some of the 7-litre engine models struggle to hit 80 mph which, on reflection, is probably just as well. However, as soon as he touches down here Hank tries his luck at speeding which, one way or another, usually lands him in deep shit.

- They have absolutely no concept of lane discipline and the principles of overtaking. They are used to travelling in whatever lane suits them, usually on cruise control, and in the US it's not unusual to see four lanes of traffic on a four-lane highway all travelling at the same speed, cavalcade fashion. The concept of using outside lanes as overtaking or fast lanes is totally alien to them.

- They have absolutely no concept of the superiority of the Volvo Driver. Sure, they have Volvos in the US but they're not common and they certainly won't be acquainted with the *Volvo Driver's Highway Code*. So they think nothing of treating the Volvo Driver like any other pesky motorist, prompting the Volvo Driver to deliver a rapid reality check.

16.12 Mr & Mrs Nissan Micra from Japan - During the 80's and 90's there was a large influx of Japanese electronics companies and car manufacturers into this country. Unfortunately this brought about a large influx of Japanese people sent here to show the local workforce how to do things Japanese-style. This often meant long contracts as a result of which whole battalions of Japanese families up-rooted and moved to the UK. With hubby spending 16 hours a day at the factory this left wifey at a loose end and looking for ways to occupy her time. Often this meant getting together with other Japanese wives and going for sightseeing trips out in her little company car, which of course will be an honourable Nissan Micra. Ah so. Now it will come as no surprise to learn that most Japanese wives rely upon their hubbies and have probably never needed to take a driving test in their native country. In fact they've probably never been allowed to. Unfortunately this certainly hasn't stopped them having a go since they will regard it as their imperial right to take a car out on the road whenever they like. Being in a foreign country makes not one jot of difference.

This does not bode well for the Volvo Driver who has already had his fill of our own Women Drivers, Learner Drivers, other Foreign Drivers and assorted nutters fouling up the highways. So if, as a Volvo Driver, you feel you have just cause don't flinch from pulling Mrs Nissan Micra over and making a citizen's arrest, demanding to see her driving licence, insurance, passport, shopping list or anything else that takes your fancy. She won't know what you're on about but if you look severe and officious enough she should be suitably intimidated. This will hopefully encourage her to nag the arse off Mr Nissan Micra to finish his contract and get the hell back to The Land of the Rising Sun.

Notes of Caution:

(1)   While you're delivering your lecture to Mrs Nissan Micra for God's sake don't lean on her car, the bodywork of which will have the metallic resistance of a Christmas decoration. The resulting damage could seriously undermine your position of authority.

(2)   Make sure Mr Plod is not in the vicinity at the time. Having to explain your perfectly democratic actions to a politically correct law enforcement android will be a pain in the butt,

        particularly if Mr Nissan Micra happens to be one of the Chief Constable's golfing partners.

16.13 Big Bad Boris, the Eastern European Juggernaut Driver - With British industry sourcing more and more materials from low-cost markets such as Eastern Europe, there has been a huge increase in haulage deliveries from these countries. These arrive as gigantic juggernauts and trailers which pour off the North Sea ferries to wreak yet more havoc for the Volvo Driver. Prominent among these juggernaut drivers is Big Bad Boris, a huge throwback to Darwin's Theory of Evolution. Big Bad Boris thrives on a diet of black coffee, adrenalin, anabolic steroid sandwiches and no sleep. His great arms grip the steering wheel as he thunders down the motorways; he is in fact a role model for the British truck driver *(see section 11)*. He is not to be argued with and nor do you need to. Most of them come to a grinding halt eventually when they realise they've never been to England before and can't read the road signs or speak the lingo to ask for directions. Should you encounter one at the side of the road you should do your best to befriend him and offer some directional help. For example, if he's looking for Bradford in West Yorkshire, direct him to Bradford-on-Avon in Wiltshire. This will give him extra experience to enable him to drive here properly. Of course, this strategy could backfire somewhat if he *is* familiar with our geography and he realises you're taking the wee-wee. You may only realise this *after* he's revved up and backed over your Volvo.

Part B: GET TO KNOW THE WAY TO DRIVE YOUR VOLVO

This part of the *Volvo Driver's Highway Code* deals with the general rules of roadcraft and driving, and how they should be interpreted by the Volvo Driver.

17. CONTROL OF YOUR CAR:

Your Volvo will be well-equipped with a whole range of features essential to the smooth and safe driving of your car. Let's look at each one and see how they can be employed to your best advantage:

17.1 Mirrors - Your Volvo has two types of mirror; a rear view mirror and wing mirrors. They should be used in the following manner:

> 1. *Rear View Mirror* - this only needs to be used rarely, if ever (unless of course you have good reason to believe that those flashing blue lights behind you are trying to tell you something). For example, while driving on a motorway, if you intend to pull out into the fast lane from the middle lane (you will not be in the inside lane which as you know is for the use of lorries, coaches and the rest of the motoring fraternity) then there's no need to look in the mirror. Simply pull out, signalling as you go, safe in the knowledge that the car speeding up in the outside lane where *you* want to be will slow down and let you in. You may then need to look in the mirror to see who's blasting their horn at you as he hits the brakes, and you may wish to acknowledge this with an appropriate hand signal.

If, on the other hand, *you* are in the outside lane and a thoughtless driver pulls out in front of *you*, then once you have got past him you should wake him (or her) up with your horn and vigorously tap your rear view mirror to remind him (or her) to be more careful in future.

2.   *Wing Mirrors* - these are to be positioned to enable you to check for hazards and dangers. Primarily these will be police patrol cars. For example, position your nearside wing mirror so that you can watch out for the inevitable jam sandwich hiding up on a motorway slip road as you cruise past below.

17.2   Lights - Your Volvo will be fitted with many different types of lighting systems, some of them not always enjoyed by lesser vehicles. Here is a summary of them, and what you should do in each case:

1.   *Side Lights / Driving Lights* - usually these will be switched on automatically when you start the car. You have no choice. Lesser vehicles will not be fitted with such safety devices and when lighting-up time approaches you should remind them of this with vigorous use of your headlamp flasher.

2.   *Headlights - Dipped Beam* - to be used in built-up areas equipped with street lamps and when driving behind police cars on motorways. In all other cases you should use:

3.   *Headlights - Full Beam* - there are two modes for using full beam; *Volvo mode* and *non-Volvo mode:*

Volvo mode - this is driving on full beam and forgetting to dip them when another vehicle is coming towards you. Ignore his flashing. He must appreciate that Volvo Drivers need to see where they're going.

Non-Volvo mode - this is when other cars drive on full beam and forget to dip them when coming towards *you.* Remind him there are Volvos on the road by blinding *him* with your full beam.

4.   *Headlights - Flashing Signals* - next to the horn the headlamp flasher is the most powerful weapon in the Volvo Driver's armoury. It should be frequently employed to ensure your safe passage at your chosen driving speed. Occasions when headlamp flashing is called for are:

•   Informing the car in front that you wish to overtake. Now.

•   One minute after lighting-up time, self-righteously informing forgetful drivers of the need to switch on *their* lights.

•   During overtaking when flashing or full beam can be used to invite on-coming vehicles to give way.

•   Greeting other Volvo Drivers and confusing everybody else at the same time.

•   Warning on-coming Volvo Drivers (nobody else) of the speed cameras / radar speed traps you've just driven through.

Occasions when you should **not** use your headlamp flashers include:

•   Letting a vehicle on the inside lane get in front of you in order to overtake a truck etc.

- Giving way to cars wanting to turn right across your path.

- Letting cars out from a side road.

5.   *Front Fog Lights* - these are ideally set to illuminate the nearside verge and the centre of the road respectively. Though primarily designed for use in fog *(see section 20.3)* they can also make very useful guiding lights should your personal visibility become impaired, for example, through reasons of fatigue.

6.   *Rear Fog Lights* - apart from their primary function of making you more visible in fog, these also make excellent spoof brake lights with which to deter tailgaters. When, for example, Boy Racer or some other nutcase is driving right up your Volvo's rear end flash the rear fog lights on and off quickly. This will give the immediate impression that you are suddenly braking, causing them to slam on their brakes. The resulting altercation, which by now you have happily left behind you, can be enhanced still further on a wet, or even better, an icy road. Maximum effect can be achieved when the tailgater is pulling a caravan *(see section 6)*.

7.   *Hazard Warning Lights* - these are to be used to alert other motorists to hazardous situations. Other occasions when you may need to use your hazard warning lights are as follows:

- Parking on yellow lines, or in some other way causing a temporary obstruction, while you nip out to the cashpoint, or do your months shopping in Sainsbury's.

- Reversing up one-way streets or motorway slip roads *(see section 18.13)*.

- Driving through "pedestrian only" precincts.

8. *Ancillary / Optional Lighting Systems* - see section 17.9.

17.3 Steering Wheel - Since Volvos are equipped with power-assisted steering (PAS) it is an easy task to manoeuvre the car using the steering wheel. So there is absolutely no need at all to glue your hands to the wheel in a vice-like grip in the traditional "ten-to-two" position. This is for Learner Drivers who have yet to learn better, the older generation who were taught to drive when cars weighed two tons and PAS was a fantasy, and PSV / lorry drivers. Think about it. You want to turn left, so what's easier? Laboriously feeding the wheel through a white-knuckled ten-to-two or nonchalantly "circling" the wheel with one hand (or even a finger), requiring hardly any effort at all? Exactly. PAS was invented for a reason and by the same principles your motorway cruising position should be holding the steering wheel on the right-hand side with your right hand and your elbow resting on the door arm-rest (what else is it for?). This leaves your left hand free to change CDs, rummage for sweets in the glove box, have a scratch, pick your nose or even guzzle a can of Coke - whatever is your pleasure. However, be aware that the local constabulary does require you to drive with both hands on the steering wheel at all times. They are therefore inclined to take a dim view of you tucking into your lunch on the hoof at 90 mph. So when that red Volvo that's been behind you for the last six miles reveals itself to be an unmarked police car containing two Old Bill who haven't even had time for a snack, do the decent thing - wind the window down and offer Mr Plod a sandwich. After all, it's only going to cost you a couple of slices of bread, some ham and six penalty points.

17.4   Gears - Gear changing is a simple feat for Volvo Drivers, particularly if the car is an automatic. The principles involved are simple. First and second gears are there for you to maintain your superiority at traffic lights, particularly if you have Boy Racer breathing down your neck. Third / fourth gears allow you to reach your cruising speeds, and fifth / sixth gears allow you to stay there, occupying your rightful place in the outside lane of the motorway *(see section 19)*. Thereafter, you should only need to change down if you genuinely feel that you need to. This may be for the following reasons:

- You actually want to stop.

- You need to turn left or right, or negotiate a roundabout, on all four wheels.

- You need overtake a Learner Driver on a steep hill without loss of speed or momentum.

- Boy Racer has caught up with you in a cloud of smoke and you need to drop down a gear to increase your acceleration and remind him of his position in life.

- Having just got past that artic that's held you up for ten miles you need to perform the imperceptible "slowing down trick" *(see section 11.3)*. Remember another of the fundamental laws of the Volvo Driver:

   "Revenge is a dish best served at 15 mph" (and with a clear road in front)

- You need that extra bit of "poke" to get past that artic and squeeze into the gap before the artic coming the other way squeezes you.

- You want to play with the kick-down on your new automatic

gearbox with the "sports" setting engaged.

- You've just gone through your third speed camera in as many miles.

- Your Volvo's computerised Information Centre has just informed you of a total brake failure.

17.5   Horn - Without doubt the most potent weapon in the Volvo Driver's armoury. This book has identified numerous examples of where use of the horn is recommended but in view of the importance of this particular piece of equipment let's just summarise them again so that there's no room for any doubt. Volvos are fitted with particularly loud horns, and occasions when they should be used include the following:

- Bringing jaywalkers and doddery old cyclists back to Planet Earth.

- Requesting the car in front not to hog the outside lane and to move over to let you pass.

- Reminding the lorry driver / JCB / tractor that you've finally managed to overtake after five miles of trying that there are other road users to consider. You.

- Informing the caravan driver that's held you up for the last twenty miles that you have formed a very low opinion of his / her general intelligence and character. You may wish to reinforce this with an appropriate hand signal *(see section 25)*.

- Alerting on-coming traffic that you are overtaking and coming through, and that consequently they should take avoiding action.

- Attracting the attention of passers-by from the ditch you've just ended up in.

- Stampeding cattle when confronted with Farmer Giles' herd wandering all over the country road that you happen to be using.

- Intimidating the car in front who is going 2 mph slower than you, and where traffic conditions prevent you from overtaking.

- Saying "hello" to the lady driver standing beside her car with a flat tyre as you whizz past (try not to smirk).

- Scaring the hell out of Learner Drivers.

17.6   Windscreen Wipers & Washers - There's not really much you can say about these. Volvo Drivers need to see where they're going just as much as any other motorist, and just like any other motorist they will be faced with the same irritating problems. For example, you will always find that the one part of the wiper blade with a nick or other imperfection, i.e. producing a semicircular smear on the windscreen, will be right in your line of vision. Do not be vexed. Stop at some convenient point such as traffic lights or at the entrance to a pay-as-you-enter car park and swap the blades over. At this point you will find that the tiny piece of grit stuck on your windscreen that caused the smear in the first place has now hacked a lump out of this other wiper blade too, putting you back to square one. Even with Volvos you will find occasions when the gods have got it in for you.

If you're driving a Volvo estate or hatchback make sure the rear wiper blade is also in good nick to enable you to keep a watchful eye for the flashing blue light brigade.

Remember also to keep the washer bottle topped up with water and a dash of washing-up liquid.

17.7   Seat Belts - These devices are fundamentally designed to protect the occupants of your Volvo in the unfortunate event of an impact. This is particularly important if the impact is caused by another Volvo. Whether or not you actually wear them is a matter for personal conscience, and there are fewer subjects guaranteed to drag everybody into a heated argument. Half the country argues that they should be worn, and the other half feels that they contravene their human rights and restricts their personal freedom. No prizes for guessing which half the insurance companies support. Whichever side of the fence you decide to land on is up to you but if you, as the Volvo Driver, do decide that your human rights and freedoms have been violated then you should be aware of two things:

- The law actually requires you to wear them. And not just in the front of the car; the passengers in the back have to wear them, too.

- Those resourceful fellows at Volvo also think you should wear them, and if you attempt to drive without putting your seat belt on you will be subjected to a barrage of flashing red lights and a monotonous ringing of bells pitched at the frequency of fingernails being drawn down a blackboard. These are the *Volvo Torture Bells.*

Seat belts are designed to basically restrict your movement, but this can have advantages *and* disadvantages as we can see:

- In the event of a front-end prang the seat belt will help to prevent you from impaling yourself on the steering column, or nutting the windscreen. But then so will the airbags. The downside of being strapped in is when you're the victim of a side impact. Even with *SIPS* and side air bags the seat belts will keep you in your seat so that you can try on the other car's radiator grille for size. If you weren't strapped in the impact could knock you clear across the car, allowing you to emerge out the other side relatively unscathed.

- Seat belts can also help with romantic liaisons when parked up in some secluded spot. For example, having got your delightful companion nicely topped up with a skinful of chardonnay and peach schnapps chasers, with a little imagination seat belts can become a very realistic substitute for handcuffs (should a little bondage be the order of the day). The downside of this is when you unwittingly overdo the peach schnapps chasers and you can't get the seat belts undone fast enough to get her out of the car before she throws up.

Rumour has it that Volvo themselves were at the forefront of developing seat belts in the first place, but one thing is certain; like most things these days they aren't half as much fun as they used to be. The original models looked as if they had been stripped from a Lancaster bomber, with great belts of criss-crossed webbing ending in a huge spring-loaded metal buckle designed to mangle the fingers of the unwary. Now you just pull the belt out of its holster in the door pillar and lock it into the retaining catch that pokes up between the seats. These are inertia-reel belts and they bring their own problems in the shape of the *Seat Belt Gremlin* that grabs the belt tight when you're half-way pulling it out and you have to let it go all the way back in and try again. After five attempts you have to catch the Seat Belt Gremlin unawares and ease it out inch by inch. Alternatively, you can relieve your own tensions by shouting *"bollocks!"* and driving off regardless, complete with flashing lights and the torture bells. You will also find that the only time you actually want the belt to go back into the holster is when you undo it to get out of the car and it just hangs there, resulting in a damaged belt and scratched paintwork as you inadvertently slam the buckle in the door.

As we have seen, the Volvo Driver is often faced with many choices, and it is one of the purposes of this book to help him make the right ones. Whether you decide to use seat belts or not is a matter of personal choice after a judicious appraisal of the risks involved. It's up to you. However, should you decide not to wear them you should consider some diversionary tactics such as the following:

- If you're driving an older model Volvo turn up the stereo to drown out the torture bells. Be careful, though, that you don't also drown out Mr Plod's sirens.

  Note of Caution: Unfortunately, on newer Volvos the torture bells are set to cut out the radio or stereo so this trick isn't going to work.

- For complete peace, before getting into the car pull the seat belt out and lock it into the retaining catch between the seats as you would normally do, and then just get into the car and sit on the seat belt. As well as de-activating the warning lights and torture bells you can also fool Mr Plod who is cruising behind you into thinking that you are actually wearing them because he will still be able to spot the belt pulled out from the door pillar. All you have to do now is pray that some nimrod doesn't unwittingly crash into you.

17.8   Miscellaneous Equipment - Your Volvo will also be fitted with many other features which are operated by a variety of knobs and switches. You will need to familiarise yourself with them and decide how you should best employ them. The equipment operated by these knobs and switches will include the following, depending upon the model you're driving:

1. *Heated Rear Window* - for clearing up a steamed up back window and is essential in order for you to observe the traffic conditions behind you, and in particular the impending approach of a Company Rep, Boy Racer or a jam sandwich.

2. *Multi-speed Fan* - essential for clearing steamed-up

windscreens and for circulating climate-controlled air in the passenger cabin of your Volvo. Unfortunately, electric fans also circulate odours, such as those emanating from farmyards or sewage disposal works on the outside, and digestive odours arising from the occupants on the inside. Sometimes it's very difficult to tell which is which.

3. *Heated Front Seats* - these are especially pleasant for warming up the leather front seats in brass monkey weather. It has been reported that heated seats can also improve the general demeanour of both driver and front seat passenger, and enhance any romantic prospects should you be using your Volvo for purposes other than going from A to B *(see section 18.14)*.

17.9   Optional Extras - Your Volvo can be fitted with a whole range of additional equipment over and above the normal specification for the model. Let's look at some of this equipment and the advantages they offer the Volvo Driver:

1. *Spotlight Systems* - for the more ambitious Volvo Driver, and are in addition to the lights fitted as standard *(see section 17.2)*. There are three general rules that must be observed if you are considering adding spotlights to your Volvo:

(1)   Spotlights should never be mounted as single lights. They must always be mounted in pairs, or as manifolds of four or even six lights.

(2)   They must be mounted on ostentatious metal frames, preferably bull-bars, and are therefore more suited to the 4x4 models.

(3)   The wattage of each light should, as a minimum, rival that of a searchlight. They can then be used to illuminate huge swathes of the road ahead along with adjacent fields, or to attract the attention of low-flying aircraft.

2.   *Flashing Blue Lights for the Radiator Grille* - these are twin blue lights mounted out of sight behind the radiator grille, one each side of the Volvo badge. When switched on they will flash alternately. It has been suggested that these lights may not be strictly legal and perhaps don't have the official blessing from Volvo Cars themselves, but nevertheless they can provide the Volvo Driver with endless hours of harmless fun. For example, you will be amazed at the reactions of a Sunday Driver, Boy Racer, or even a 44-tonne truck that's been getting on your nerves, when you approach them from behind and suddenly switch on the blue lights, thus simulating the actions of an unmarked jam sandwich.

There are, however, a few small drawbacks which must be taken into consideration if you are thinking of having these blue lights fitted. For example:

● You will have to fit them yourself since Volvo workshops will be unable or unwilling to do the job for you. Either that, or seek out the services of one of the many excellent exclusive little workshops that can be found operating out of back street lock-ups or under railway arches in most towns, and where cash-in-hand is appreciated, no questions asked.

● You may well fall foul of Mr Plod if he catches you using them. A tried and tested way out of this is to claim that they were already fitted to the car when you bought it, and that you've just found the switch and was wondering what it was for. (Well, what *does* happen to jam sandwiches once they've been pensioned off?).

- You could invalidate your Volvo warranty which could come back to haunt you when, for example, the mechanic that you've employed to fit the lights manages to screw up your Volvo's entire electrical system.

3.   *Sunroof* - as the name suggests, the prime function of a sunroof is to let in sunlight and fresh air. However, for the Volvo Driver, a sunroof also makes an excellent aperture for the following activities:

- Conveying hand signals to lorry drivers. Since drivers of artics and other large trucks are perched high above the roof of your Volvo they're not really going to be able to see any hand signals that you may care to make in the conventional manner, i.e. through your side window . But they can see the sunroof. So, having been subjected to some of the tricks of the lorry driver's trade *(see section 11)* you may feel it appropriate to convey your sentiments with a hand signal such as those illustrated in section 25 of this book, and the sunroof offers the ideal facility. Before doing so, however, you would be wise to make sure that you have a clear open road in front of you at the time to make good your escape.

- Sticking your head through to admire, and perhaps even photograph, areas of outstanding natural beauty or famous landmarks such as Stonehenge, the Angel of the North, or a Volvo showroom packed full of the latest models. Obviously, you would not attempt to do this while driving. Pull over to the side of the road, or wait until you get held up at the next set of traffic lights.

Environmental Tip: - sunroofs are definitely NOT to be used for the disposal of lighted cigarette ends, coke cans, empty crisp packets and other litter. Such actions are considered to be extremely anti-social and could seriously tarnish the image of the Volvo Driver - particularly if the discarded rubbish lands on a jam sandwich.

4. *Reversing Sensors* - officially called a "Park Assist Facility" these are radar-operated sensors fitted to the Volvo's rear bumper. When reversing these sensors emit a series of beeps which get closer together as you close in on an obstacle such as a wall or another car. The beeps change to a continuous sound just before the moment of impact.

Reversing sensors were designed primarily to assist the lady driver who thinks she can reverse a Volvo (ha! ha!). The following are therefore considered to be very relevant points:

- The system pays for itself very quickly, as the cost of fitting reversing sensors is considerably less than the average rear end repair bill from a Volvo bodyshop.

- It is widely rumoured that the insurance companies are seriously considering adding a supplement to the annual insurance premium of lady drivers who don't have reversing sensors fitted to their Volvos. More power to their elbow.

When you think about it why stop at just reversing sensors? It would be a lot more practical for the lady driver if these sensors were extended around all four sides of the car. This would at least give other obstacles such as the car in front, your garage walls, or an oak tree *(see section 18.13)* a bit more of a fighting chance.

5.   *Electric Folding Wing Mirrors* - the Volvo Driver can now have electric controls fitted which, at the touch of a switch, folds your wing mirrors in against the body of the car. This can be an especially useful accessory when:

●   attempting to navigate narrow gaps with walls on each side;

●   cutting it a bit fine when overtaking;

●   in the car wash, where there may be a serious risk of the washer mechanism removing folded-out wing mirrors altogether.

6.   *Satellite Navigation / Global Positioning Systems (GPS)* - fitted as standard to the top-of-the-range models, otherwise they are seriously pricey accessories. GPS will enable you to plan the best route for your journey, calculate the mileage, and show your exact location at any time - all working from a pre-programmed CD and using a small television screen. If you switch it to audio you can also be given a running commentary on your journey by a Dalek with a bad head cold as you proceed on your way, though some Volvo Drivers may find this distracting. GPS is also placid and is programmed not to bust a fuse when the Volvo Driver, in a rare moment of mischief, deliberately takes a wrong turning just to see how the GPS reacts. GPS is only really essential should you find yourself in the following critical situations:

●   When you're navigating your way through a strange or unfamiliar part of town or countryside, and you have no accurate maps to hand.

● When you have the maps, but these are being read by your lady passenger upon whom you are relying as your navigator.

Note of Caution: GPS systems are multi-national, so make sure you've installed the correct CD for the country you're in. Trying to navigate your way around Sheffield's one-way systems while being instructed in Serbo-Croat can upset one's mental compass.

7. *In-Car TV and Entertainment Systems* - as for GPS systems these are fitted as standard to the top-of-the-range models, otherwise they are available as optional accessories. For obvious reasons the TV won't work while the car is moving, but it does provide at-seat entertainment when you're stationary. For example, you can tune in to the football results while holed up in a multi-storey car park awaiting the return of the wife from one of her shopping marathons. Or if you're parked up in some secluded spot with a romantic companion there's nothing like a 30-minute burst of *"East Enders"* to set the mood.

It is appreciated, however, that in-car TV will not suit all tastes. So if the TV is not to your liking the Dolby stereo system can provide all the music you need from the radio or multi-change CD player.

Note of Caution: If you are comfortably settled in a secluded spot don't overstay your welcome. Hours of TV and /or music can quietly drain all the juice out of your Volvo's electrics and this will not become apparent until much later when you try and start the car - only to find the battery is as flat as a pancake. This could have potentially embarrassing repercussions if, for example, your romantic companion had no business being with you in the first place.

17.10 The Magic Touch - Up until now we've had a good look at the main features and controls of your Volvo, most of which are fitted as standard though some are available as optional extras, depending upon the model you're driving. And there are always new developments and ideas being tried out, particularly with the continual progress in computer and in-car technology. There are, however, worrying signs that the Volvo is slowly developing a mind of its own and that the boffins in Volvo Development are losing the plot. How else can we explain the increasing ability of the car to think for itself and even to anticipate what you, the Volvo Driver, is planning to do (or more alarmingly, what the car thinks you **ought** to do), and then promptly do it first? I tell you, we are witnessing the first stages of the "Rise of the Swedish Machines". You don't think so? Well, consider the following examples of features now fitted as standard to some new Volvos:

1.   *Rain Sensors* - once upon a time when it rained you switched the wipers on. Now, as if by magic, the bloody things switch themselves on at the first signs of moisture. We are reliably informed that this is due to a new microchip hidden in the windscreen behind the rear view mirror that detects water and sends a signal to the wipers when in intermittent mode. And of course they can't be disconnected or over-ridden, so you're stuck with them. They are so obviously a very valuable feature, especially when they are activated by a lorry chucking up muck from a wet road, it's stopped raining, and your washer bottle needs re-filling.

2.   *Auto-dimming Rear View Mirror* - instead of having a manual anti-glare setting which you manipulate yourself, your rear view mirror now dims itself when faced with what it decides is too much glare from the headlights of the vehicles

behind. The trouble is that nobody seems to know what "too much glare" is, so if the glare factor is set too low dipped

headlights resemble a torch bulb in the mirror, and flashing blue lights can't be seen at all.

If we are to accept that the car is gradually taking over our minds then why not adopt a "if you can't beat 'em, join 'em" approach and put our own suggestions forward for automating the car to the Volvo boffins. Instead of gimmicks let's recommend some developments that would *really* be of use. The following spring immediately to mind:

- Radar sensors which can spot a speed camera before it spots you and automatically decreases your speed.

- Perfume sensors that automatically detect when a lady is trying to drive your Volvo, and engages the immobiliser.

- A radio that automatically switches itself off when a Cliff Richard record is played.

- A GPS audio system that automatically argues with the wife, the mother-in-law or any other back seat driver - and wins.

17.11 Vehicle Security - As a Volvo Driver you are aware of the prestige that you bring to the roads, and consequently of the envy this induces in lesser road users. For reasons best known to themselves some of these people actually nurture a deep resentment against Volvo Drivers and complain bitterly whenever a Volvo glides past them on the motorway. Sometimes this is reinforced with impotent gestures of defiance. The only way to respond to this petulance is by giving the offender the look that unmistakeably says *"Yes, that's right, I do have a better car than yours. Deal with it"*. Unfortunately this often results in road rage and in extreme cases it can provoke acts of wanton vandalism against the Volvo Driver who has to accept that, because he drives a Volvo, he's going to be a target for all sorts of ne'er-do-wells and social misfits. To try and combat this a whole range of security devices are available that will at least go some way towards deterring the casual car thief, hub-cap collector or general hooligan. For example, your Volvo will be fitted with the following devices as standard:

- Remote-control deadlocks for the doors which prevent the doors from being opened from the inside after the passage of a large rock through one of the windows.

- An alarm system, set to activate if the car is disturbed. This also generates much fun for small boys who delight in rocking the car to see how loud the alarm is.

- An immobiliser which prevents the car from being started. Unfortunately it doesn't prevent the car from being lifted up and whisked away on a trailer.

- Locking wheel nuts to protect your alloys and reduce the chances of you returning from a shopping trip to find your Volvo resting on four piles of bricks, the wheels nowhere to be found. Just make sure that you carry the wheel nut adapter in a secret place in your Volvo (but not so secret that you can't find it when you get that puncture deep in the countryside on a wet November night).

There are also other security devices on the market which you can either fit yourself or have Volvo do it for you; for example the steering wheel lock and the gear lever lock. Both have their uses in deterring the chancer but to a professional armed with bolt-cutters they're chicken feed.

Fortunately, there are other measures which you can take to protect your Volvo though some of these are, shall we say, a little unorthodox.

But these are lawless times and desperate measures are often called for. It's no good expecting Mr Plod to be patrolling the streets as a figure of authority - he and his mates will all be staked out on the by-pass manning a speed trap. So here are some additional vehicle security ideas for your consideration:

- Electrifying the body shell of the car from the battery. If the car is touched the miscreant gets a shocking surprise. Breaks the ice at parties.

- A dust-gun filled with flour with the nozzle hidden in an air vent at face level. As soon as the ignition is switched on the would-be tea-leaf gets a blast of flour right in the face. For added effect use itching powder or carbon dust instead of flour. Breaks the ice at kiddies' parties. (Just make sure you de-activate the device before *you* get in to drive your car).

- Clamp your own wheels when parked.

  Note for lady drivers: if it's your own clamp you've fitted you do *not* need to call out a cowboy clamping firm to release it for a fee of £150. You will actually have a key to do this yourself.

- Install a speaking alarm system. When activated a high-pitched hysterical female voice will announce to the world in an American accent: *"Help, I'm being stolen! Help, I'm being stolen!..."*. For the Volvo Driver used to the more sophisticated things in life this is undoubtedly naff, but it is surprisingly effective. You can inject a bit more fun into the proceedings if you happen to know an electronics whizz-kid who can change the alarm's vocal warning. Try to imagine a traffic warden accidentally activating the alarm as he / she slaps a ticket on your windscreen and being greeted with *"You're an asshole! You're an asshole! You're an asshole!...."* at 200 decibels.

18.   DRIVING TECHNIQUES - USING THE ROAD:

18.1   Moving off / pulling out - When pulling out from a parked position against the pavement remember that you have the right of way over on-coming traffic. Your pulling-out procedure should therefore follow a 4-stage process, as follows:

Stage 1   Pull out.

Stage 2   Adjust the rear view mirror to observe the car behind
                    you standing on its front bumper.

Stage 3   Signal to indicate that you've just pulled out.

Stage 4   Slow down to a speed just below that of the car behind
                    you. He (or she) needs to learn that if he / she hadn't
                    been driving so fast in the first place he / she wouldn't
                    have had to brake so sharply when you pulled out.

18.2   Once moving - As you drive down the road maintain your speed to 2 mph under the speed limit. This will remind the other more reckless road users of the lawful speed limits. Emphasise this by keeping well to the centre of the road, thus reducing the risk of you being overtaken by some lunatic.

The law requires you to keep both hands on the wheel at *all* times. It is important to remember this since there have been instances of prosecutions arising from motorists seen driving with only one hand on the wheel. You must therefore ensure that you always have a passenger with you to change gear, operate the heater controls, switch on windscreen wipers etc.

18.3   Signalling / Indicating - Part of making your journey as smooth as possible is the assurance of knowing that other road users will always signal their intention to overtake, turn left or turn right, and of course to cancel the indicators after use to avoid confusion. You will of course always come across the absent-minded or downright inconsiderate motorist who doesn't signal and expects you to rely upon your psychic powers to read his (or her) intentions. Such people must be reminded of their obligations to other road users through a serious burst on the horn.

The other side of the coin is ensuring correct use of the indicators when *you* are driving your Volvo. Here we go back to basics. Fundamentally, your journey and the route you decide to take are your business and nobody else's. There is, therefore, absolutely no reason to show anybody else what you're doing by indicating. After all, you know where you're going, don't you? However, bear in mind that the following situations may call for indicating, depending of course upon the frame of mind you happen to find yourself in at the time:

- Turning left - *see section 18.9*
- Turning right - *see section 18.8*
- Overtaking - *see section 18.5*
- Pulling out - *see section 18.1*
- Negotiating roundabouts - *see section 18.10*

Remember that your indicators are intended to let other road users know what you plan to do. However, there may be some instances when you can't decide what to do, for example at T-junctions where there isn't an adequate directional signpost. Turn left or turn right? Indicate your intention by switching on your hazard warning lights. This will signify that you could be turning in either direction or even turning in both directions at once. Then drive off in your chosen direction leaving the car behind to figure out what those hazards actually were.

On the rare occasion that you do signal to overtake or turn right remember to leave your indicators on to let everybody know that you might want to overtake or turn right again sometime before the end of your journey. You will also find that this is an excellent way of attracting attention to yourself, for example, on the day after your tax disc expires.

18.4   Speed Limits - As you cruise along in your Volvo you must be mindful of the varying speeds limits that apply to each stretch of road. This is especially important when you consider the speed cameras that have saturated the country. The following considerations are therefore important to the Volvo Driver:

1.   *Speed Limit Variations* - these are many, and can be very confusing for the Volvo Driver on a tight schedule. You will need to bear the following in mind:

(1)   The maximum speed limit for motorways is 70 mph, which equates to 90 mph on a Volvo speedometer. This is therefore the maximum speed you should drive at. However you must remain vigilant for sudden hazards which may require you to slow down. These hazards can include patchy fog, wet or icy roads, flashing blue lights etc.

(2)   In built-up areas the maximum speed limit is 30 mph. This is therefore the speed at which the Volvo Driver should travel, regardless of parked cars, speed humps, Lollipop Persons, old ladies crossing the road, and other obstacles designed to impede your progress.

(3)   Where children are likely to be in the vicinity, for example near schools or playing on the roads on sink estates, some local authorities have created 20 mph zones. These may be reinforced with speed humps or some other type of traffic calming measure (*see section 18.15*). The justification for this is that by forcing the Volvo Driver to travel no faster than 20 mph, it makes

the roads safer for the children. However, it can be argued that children have no business playing on the road in the first place when there are perfectly good bus shelters and telephone boxes to vandalise. It can also be argued that, at 20 mph, your Volvo presents a much easier target for the children's welcoming barrage of bricks, stones and bottles.

(4)   There will also be special cases where speeds are temporarily restricted, most notably in contraflow sections of road works. We will deal with this later in our section on Road Works (section 22).

2.   *Speed Cameras* - contrary to the Official Party Line, speed cameras have absolutely nothing to do with reducing accidents and saving lives, and everything to do with raising revenue for the local authority and Mr Plod to squander. This has been the case ever since the Police Authorities were given the green light by central government to keep the lion's share of fines extorted from speeding motorists. Anybody telling you anything different is either clinically delusional, a bare-faced liar, or a politician - or possibly a combination of all three.

Now, no sane person will condone driving at dangerously excessive speeds, but let's get this into perspective. There is a world of difference between driving at 90 mph on a wet motorway and nudging 32 mph in a built-up area on a dry sunny day. They are both technically "speeding" but the speed camera is unable to distinguish between the two, or make any allowances for circumstances or road conditions etc. So the hapless motorist gets gleefully clobbered and the local Police Authority trousers most of the fine - to be spent on installing more cameras. It wouldn't appear quite so cynical if the cameras were actually sited at accident black spots but apparently more than half of them are located on safe roads with low accident rates.

It is also possible to lose your licence on one journey if you shoot past enough cameras. As a Volvo Driver you have a duty to set the standards for other road users to follow. Therefore, should you find yourself on the receiving end of, say, six speeding tickets in one journey you should offer the following mitigating circumstances in your defence:

•   You were **not** speeding six times. You were speeding **once** (you didn't slow down). You just had your picture taken six times.

•   A speed camera is a measuring device and as such should be subject to regular calibration against known standards. Ask to see details of the Police Authority calibration programme and the results of the last calibration of the camera(s) that nailed you. Chances are Mr Plod won't know what the hell you're talking about, which will be music to the ears of a ruthless defence lawyer.

If all else fails, plead insanity.

3.   *Speed Indicator Signs* -   there is now another distraction for the Volvo Driver to take in - the electronic speed indicator sign. These are becoming more popular in both urban and rural areas, and Norfolk in particular seems to have more than its fair share of them disfiguring the countryside at the approach to villages. The signs appear on square boards which are mounted on poles near speed control zones and are set to flash a message to the on-coming Volvo driver regarding his perceived speed. Triggered by radar aimed at you as you approach the speed zone, your perceived speed is

transformed into a message which lights up in pretty colours. The content of the messages can vary, from actually telling you what your speed is (31 mph, 42 mph etc), to nagging you with *"Slow down"* or *"Too fast"*. Because the Volvo Driver is so aware of the dangers associated with distractions like these, he would be quite justified in taking exception to these impertinent electronic monstrosities and seek answers to the following questions:

(1)   Since these signs are announcing your approach speed to the world at large what proof is there that the figures are correct? When was the device last calibrated, and by whom *(see section 18.4.2)*?

(2)   If the signs flash up the message *"Too fast"* to what does this relate? Too fast for what? Milk floats? Porsche 911s? Old ladies in their Morris 1000s?

So as the coloured screen suddenly flashes up in front of him the Volvo Driver could be forgiven for succumbing to temptation and offering an appropriate acknowledgement to the sign which may or may not require the use of all fingers of the hand. This hand signal, together with a record of your speed, is then digitally captured and preserved by the camera hiding behind the screen which is now pointing at you as you drive past.

4.   *Cruise Control* - after joining a motorway, and you have assumed your rightful place in the outside lane, you will be in a position to dictate the speed of the other vehicles in that lane. Should you find yourself enjoying the rare luxury of a clear run you will not need to keep accelerating and slowing down; nor do you want to drive for miles with your foot pressed firmly against the accelerator pedal, inducing cramp

and muscle fatigue. You can maintain a smooth even pace at your chosen speed by engaging your Volvo's cruise control. This facility will automatically drive the car for you at a set speed but you do need to be careful and not get lulled into a false sense of security. You should bear the following in mind when using cruise control:

- Setting your speed at 90 mph is not recommended. Even if the rest of the traffic in your lane is going this fast when you engage the cruise control you will find that eventually most of it will slow down, switch lanes or leave the motorway altogether at some point, leaving you belting down the outside lane on your own. This will make you a conspicuous target for Mr Plod.

- Don't set the speed too slow, either, or you will be forever changing lanes as faster traffic tries to overtake you. The result of this will be the cruise control going on and off like a dud striplight, which tends to reduce its usefulness as a device for controlling cruising speeds.

- Cruise control is *not* an auto-pilot and it won't steer the car. So resist the temptation to set the cruising speed and put your feet up and watch the world go by. This can often end with the Volvo Driver watching the world go by from an upside-down perspective. As we have seen previously in section 17.3 you must keep your hands on the steering wheel at all times, not only because this is where Mr Plod expects them to be, but this is also where the control buttons for the cruise control are. Also, since touching the brake is an instantaneous way to disengage the cruise control, this is another sound reason for keeping your feet around the region of the pedals.

18.5   Overtaking - As a Volvo Driver you will appreciate that only you travel at the correct speed. Everybody else either drives either too slowly or too fast. This makes for potentially frustrating journeys when you will be constantly looking to get past slower drivers and possibly some drivers actually trying to get past you. No-one ever seems to leave you alone to cruise along unhindered. You will understand that not only do you have the right to overtake anything that is hindering your journey but you also have a public duty to prevent any nutcase from overtaking *you*, and especially if they endanger you in the process. The Volvo Driver must therefore observe the following basic rules regarding overtaking:

- Before overtaking make sure that you have the room to do so safely. Safely for you, that is.

- Move up to the vehicle you intend to overtake. This must be done carefully to ensure that you leave the right amount of space:

  - not too close; i.e. don't tailgate. You know you can stop quick-smart but the nutcase behind might not be able to. Don't run the risk of scratching your Volvo as he bounces off your rear end.

  - not too far away. The nutcase behind you may see this gap as something *he* can squeeze into. If he tries it just move up leaving him in no-man's land.

- Now pull out to the centre of the road. Flash your headlights and / or blast your horn to alert the vehicle in front that he needs to make way and let you overtake. On no account use your indicators at this point. You know you're going to overtake and, frankly, it's nobody else's business. Besides, the nutcase behind you might think that you actually intend to turn right off the road and start to move up on your inside.

You will then have to go the trouble of correcting this illusion by encouraging him to turn **left** off the road - and if there does actually happen to be a turning for him to turn into so much the better.

- As soon as it is safe to do so, overtake. "Safe to do so" is defined as ensuring that any on-coming vehicles have enough time to pull over and let you through. It is advisable at this point to hold your full-beam headlight on as you overtake to ensure that the on-coming vehicles know exactly what you intend to do.

- As you draw level with the vehicle you are overtaking indicate to let everybody know what you're doing.

- Once past him you should then pull back onto your side of the road and settle down to a cruising speed exactly that of the vehicle you've just overtaken. He will probably be wondering why the hell you bothered in the first place but then he won't appreciate the smug satisfaction you've just experienced by showing another motorist who's boss.

18.6   Slowing Down and Stopping - It's very easy to get started and build up a nice cruising speed for your journey, particularly on a dual carriageway or motorway. Unfortunately, with the sheer volume of traffic on the roads these days, coupled with the many obstacles that you're likely to face during the course of your journey, this won't last. Somebody or something is always lying in wait for you to make you slow down or even stop you altogether. Your journey can therefore be a frustrating sequence of accelerating, braking, accelerating, slowing down, stopping, starting up again, ad nauseum. Accelerating in your Volvo is easy; down goes the foot and you're away. But slowing down takes a little more skill and thought. For example, do you brake, and if so gently or sharply? Or is it sufficient to just slow down, using gentle braking and possibly the gears? No two sets of circumstances will be the same so the Volvo Driver must be prepared for any eventuality. Let's look at each action in turn, and what the implications may be for each one:

1. *Slowing Down* - you may be called upon to slow down for many reasons. Here are a few prime examples:

- As a first step when you actually need to stop the car *(see section 18.6.2)*.

- Negotiating bends, turnings, roundabouts and other obstacles on all four wheels.

- You have no choice; you're suddenly stuck behind one of those inferior vehicles / drivers that make driving such a delight. Tractors, learner drivers, buses, elderly drivers, JCBs, all manner of trucks and lorries..... the list is endless.

- The contraflow or road works that you've just driven into has a 50 mph speed limit.

- You've just spotted the speed camera or speed camera warning signs.

- You have spotted, in the nick of time, the jam sandwich that wants to get past you.

- Negotiating obstacles which can remove the underside of your Volvo if you don't slow down; e.g. hump-back bridges, severe dips on country roads, urban speed humps etc.

- Adverse weather conditions; ice, snow, high winds.

- Approaching speed limit zones.

2. *Stopping* - you may need to stop your Volvo for many reasons. For example:

- You've actually reached the end of your journey.

- You've arrived at a crossroads or T-junction and need to consult the signposts.

- The traffic lights are on red, and there's a camera on the top.

- Mr Plod's lights are flashing blue and requests the pleasure of your company.

- You've no choice - you've just got yourself snarled up in the mother of all traffic jams.

- You need to fill up with petrol and / or stock up with munchies and cans of pop for your journey.

- You need to answer that call of nature.

- You've arrived at a pedestrian crossing which may or may not be guarded by a Lollipop Person *(see section 18.11)*.

- You've arrived at a toll plaza for the Tyne Tunnel, Humber Bridge etc.

- You've got a puncture.

- You've broken down (though not in a Volvo, surely?).

3.   *Stopping Distances* - coupled with driving speeds you must always ensure that you maintain an adequate distance between yourself and the car in front so that in the event of an emergency you can safely stop without using the back end of the vehicle in front as a set of buffers. In performing safe stops the Volvo driver must remember the following:

•   You can stop on a 10-pence piece. Can the vehicle behind you do the same? Leave enough room for you to move up after braking if necessary. This is particularly important if the vehicle behind is a 44-tonne truck or a petrol tanker.

•   Handbrakes turns don't count as a means of avoiding the vehicle in front.

•   Nor does driving off the road into an escape lane (assuming there is one).

18.7   Road Junctions - We have covered some aspects of what to do when faced with road junctions in other sections of this book; for example section 18.3 tells you what you need to do when faced with a T-junction. Other sections will cover turning left or turning right. However, there are a few other types of specially-contrived obstacles posing as "road junctions" which the Volvo Driver must be able to negotiate and these are listed below. Remember that in all cases it is the over-riding objective of local councils to make life as difficult as possible for the motorist by buggering up road systems that once flowed quite effectively. For example, we have:

1.   *Box Junctions* - those familiar huge boxes of framed yellow hatchings you find painted all over the roads. It is a common fallacy that vehicles must not stop in box junctions and that they must be kept clear at all times. In actual fact they exist to provide the Volvo Driver with some much-needed

space in which to turn around should the traffic conditions become intolerable.

2.   *Mini-roundabouts* - painted on the road. These are **not** there to carefully circumnavigate like some great mechanical fairy; these are there to drive straight over. You should, however, be mindful of the rules governing priorities on roundabouts, just in case some chancer decides to dispute this with you *(see section 18.10)*.

Note of Caution: Some of the smarty-pants at the local Town Halls have designed these mini-roundabouts to be raised above the level of the road surface - some quite deceptively so that any motorist treating them as normal and driving straight across them runs a serious risk of either losing the exhaust system, petrol tank or just becoming hilariously poised on the centre. As a Volvo Driver you would obviously not want this to happen to you so it is always a good idea to give the roundabout a quick visual once-over as you approach it to judge whether you can safely drive over it or whether you will have to go round it in the usual boring fashion. It is also quite amusing watching a 44-tonne artic trying to negotiate what is essentially a ten-feet wide circular blob of white paint in the middle of a town centre; unless of course you happen to be stuck behind it.

3.   *Multi-mini-roundabouts* - again painted on the road. These are actually the brainchild of some of the less gifted Town Hall employees. The design of these features is based upon a Chinese puzzle, and makes the same amount of sense to the Volvo Driver. You see, when approaching these multi-directional patterns, nobody is really sure who has the ultimate right of way. Once you have negotiated one painted circle you find yourself on another one and the whole scenario is repeated. Frankly, the Volvo Driver's best bet is to go for it and drive

straight across the whole damned lot in one go, regardless. Everybody else will be so amazed at your assertiveness they will all stop and let you through. This is, of course, subject to two provisos:

> (1)   The *Note of Caution* above regarding raised roundabouts;

> (2)   That some of the other vehicles involved are not juggernauts, double-decker buses, car transporters or other vehicles on the larger side who don't give a damn. And police cars.

18.8   Turning Right - Turning right may or may not involve the use of traffic lights *(see section 18.12)*, depending upon whether you are leaving or joining a major road:

> 1.   *Turning right off a main road into a side road* - if you intend to turn right *off* a main road into a side road you should adopt the following procedure:

- At the junction of the road you want to turn into position yourself in the centre of the road and indicate to turn right.

- If there are traffic lights and your right turn is controlled by a filter arrow then there is not much you can do other than wait your turn.

- If, however, there is no filter arrow, or your right turn isn't controlled by lights at all then it's every man for himself as far as the Volvo Driver is concerned. The on-coming traffic isn't going to give way so you're going to have to make them.

- Do this by edging slowly across the bows of the on-coming traffic until someone is forced to give way. He / she may not like having to give way but, tough, you're driving a Volvo. Be careful, though - some drivers are pig-headed and may regard this as a challenge, and you really don't need to start playing chicken with a Boy Racer, Company Rep, or a psychotic lady driver in the grip of her hormones.

- It's a pound to a penny that the person you have made give way to let you across may express some mild frustration or even irritation at being made to stop when he / she has right of way, and by a Volvo Driver as well. Therefore, how you thank this person for giving way to you should be influenced by the type of driver and vehicle involved:

  - if it's another Volvo Driver he will understand your needs so wave cheerily and smile a big "thank you";

  - if it's a man in a different type of car look condescendingly at him and raise your hand (**all** fingers) in a gesture of thanks;

  - if it's anybody driving a Del-Boy 3-Wheeler just glare with an *"I should think so, too"* look;

  - if it's a lady driver of mature years just nod and raise your hand and try not to look too patronising;

  - if it's a young lady driver you are likely to provoke a mild attack of road rage because they are so unpredictable. If it's PMT-fuelled road rage you may have chosen unwisely. Try and defuse the situation by smiling and mouthing a "thank you" thereby preserving the reputation of the Volvo Driver as the knight of the road;

-        if you can sense that the young lady in question is a raving feminist and therefore thinks all men are bastards (especially Volvo Drivers), respond by blowing her a big wet kiss to put her in the right frame of mind for the rest of her journey. If she's PMT-fuelled as well the results could be spectacular.

-        if it's a Learner Driver, who will by now be shaking like a jelly in a wind tunnel as a result of your assertive actions, just shrug your shoulders and raise your eyebrows in a *"well, what did you expect me to do?"* look. Ignore the fist-waving and mouthed obscenities from the instructor as he peels his nose off the windscreen - he needs to concentrate on educating his pupil in the ways of the Volvo Driver.

-        if it's **anybody** pulling a caravan, ignore them. They shouldn't have been on the road in the first place.

2.   *Turning right onto a main road from a side road* - if you intend to turn right **onto** a main road out of a side road in your Volvo you should adopt the following procedure:

•   Approach the junction and stop so that you can assess the traffic flow on the main road. Remember that you're trying to drive straight across a lane (or lanes) of on-coming traffic in order to join the traffic flow on the far side, so some degree of judgement and restraint is necessary.

•   It is also a good idea on this occasion to signal right so that the on-coming traffic at least has a fair idea of what you're trying to do.

- In view of the impatient attitudes of some of today's drivers you would be advised not to just pull straight out across the stream of traffic on your side of the road in the misguided belief that these other drivers will simply stop. You will need to give these vehicles a little bit of breathing space, so pull out gradually.

- Edge forward, forcing the on-coming vehicles to swerve round you in an ever-increasing arc until one of them has no choice but to stop. As if by magic, you will then find that the traffic in the lane that you want to join on the far side of the road will also give way and let you in once they see that you're jamming up half of the road system.

Note of Caution: Unfortunately, there are still a few misguided individuals who insist upon disputing the right of way with the Volvo Driver. Unfortunately (again) these individuals tend to be driving fully-laden petrol tankers, skip lorries and the like, and with whom it would be unwise to engage in territorial disputes.

18.9 Turning Left - This very simple manoeuvre seems to be unnecessarily complicated by the Standard Highway Code. For example, it concerns itself with such trivialities such as "right of way" and "indicating". When you are driving your Volvo there is only one right of way - yours. Unfortunately this is not drummed home enough during driving lessons as a result of which you will occasionally come across an individual who will, foolishly, dispute the right of way with you. As for indicating, why wear out your flasher bulbs unduly? They cost good money to replace and, after all, *you* know where you're going. Your techniques for turning left will depend upon whether you're turning ***off*** a main road into a side road, or turning ***onto*** one from a side road. You should therefore follow these simple rules:

1.   *Turning left off a main road into a side road* - approach the turning and slow down by changing down the gearbox. Don't brake or else it will give the person behind you a clue as to what you propose to do. (If you have an automatic then of course you will have to brake; but do so at the last minute). Then turn into the side road, indicating as you do so. This will tell the person trying to turn ***out*** of the side road onto the main road (having spent the last five minutes impatiently waiting for a chance to pull out) that you have turned in. Ignore his gesticulations or general lack of coolness as he misses his chance to shoot into the gap you've just created - he should be more assertive and would never make a Volvo Driver.

2.   *Turning left onto a main road from a side road* - as before *(see section 18.8)* approach the junction and slow down to assess the traffic flow on the main road. There's no point in indicating - the traffic approaching you from the right can't see your left indicator anyway and anybody behind you who hasn't guessed by now the direction you propose to take has no business being behind the wheel of a car. Don't bother waiting for a suitable gap. You have a Volvo. Create your own space. Simply pull out and join the traffic on the main road safe in the knowledge that the car you have just pulled out in front of has two stark choices to make - miss you or hit you. He won't want to hit you, especially a Volvo, because of the damage it will do to his car. So he misses you. He does this by having to brake, and if he has to brake too sharply then he was almost certainly driving too fast and deserves the car behind him bouncing off his towbar. Then simply proceed on your way.

Note of Caution: As we have seen when turning right onto a main road from a side road *(section 18.8)* not everybody shares the philosophy of the Volvo Driver's Highway Code, so there **will** be times when it is advisable **not** to pull straight out onto the main road without first determining whether there is adequate space for you to do so. Such occasions will include:

- when the driver of the on-coming car is bigger than you;

- when the on-coming car is a police car;

- when the on-coming vehicle is a double-decker bus, a juggernaut, a car transporter or similar heavy vehicle, none of which are noted for their ability (or inclination) to stop sharply.

18.10 Roundabouts - The golden rule of roundabouts is that the vehicle on the roundabout always has right of way over vehicles approaching it. This rule could almost have been made with the Volvo Driver in mind. It therefore follows that in order for you, the Volvo Driver, to enjoy unhindered progress you need to get onto that roundabout as soon as possible. Once there you can go round and round until you decide upon the exit road you want to take. But actually getting onto the roundabout in the first place can be fraught with obstacles, not the least being the line of traffic you're stuck in while waiting your turn to get there. There is a simple ploy used by the Volvo Driver to overcome this.

Assuming that you're stuck in a line of traffic you will be aware that at the roundabout this line of traffic usually splits into two lanes; the nearside for vehicles leaving the roundabout at exits 1 and 2, (i.e. the first two off to the left), and the outside lane for those needing exits 3, 4, 5 etc. Well, that's the theory of it anyway. Your journey requires you to exit at the first road off to the left (exit 1); in other words getting onto the roundabout and then leaving it again to the left almost immediately. No problem. All you do is whizz up the outside lane past all the other waiting traffic, signalling right as you do so, and drive onto the roundabout as if you're going to exit at 3 or 4 etc. But don't - just stay on the roundabout and drive all the way round in a 360 degree circle until you reach exit 1 again and drive off. As you drive round the roundabout you will of course have the right of way over those conformist nerds still waiting in line on the approach to the roundabout - and who are now mouthing obscenities at seeing you sweep past their bows unhindered. Don't worry; they're only jealous because they haven't had the benefit of Volvo training. Illegal? No. Cheeky? No. Resourceful? Definitely. And proves again that the tactical acumen of the Volvo Driver is without equal.

Note: Mini-roundabouts and multi-mini-roundabouts have been covered in section 18.7.

18.11 Pedestrian Crossings - Hark back to one of the fundamental laws of the Volvo Driver in section 2:

"So many pedestrians. So little time"

There are two types of pedestrian crossing; those that are unmanned and those that are manned with crossing patrols. Let's now look at each type and consider the actions the Volvo Driver should take:

> 1. *Unmanned Crossings* - when pedestrians are using the pavement, as they should be, you can't touch them. Nor indeed do you need to. They are in the right place, filing along on their designated strip of paving stones while you have the freedom of the road. However, sometimes the pedestrian actually wants to get to the opposite pavement and, in the absence of subways, this means **crossing your road**. Now they're fair game. They will use designated crossing points, usually pelican or zebra crossings where they feel they enjoy

a certain amount of immunity from the Volvo Driver. Big mistake. When stopped at a crossing creep silently up to the edge of the crossing and register your disapproval at having been halted in your tracks by revving your engine like the starting grid at Monza. Just remember to take the car out of gear first. Having to peel people off your radiator grille is not only embarrassing but may also result in you taking an unscheduled holiday break at Her Majesty's Pleasure.

2.   *Manned Crossings / Crossing Patrols* - this is where the pedestrian gets a bit of back-up in his / her quest to get from one side of your road to the other in one piece. This back-up manifests itself in the form of an awesome creature called a "Lollipop Person". *(This Person is more popularly known as a Lollipop Lady since it's usually a lady that does the job, but in these enlightened days of enforced sexual equality one must conform, so - "Lollipop Person" it is).*

Now, the Lollipop Person's original purpose in life was to help schoolchildren cross the road safely, but these days their remit has been extended and they can often be seen helping other people as well. Should the Volvo Driver find himself driving anywhere near a school he should be on a constant lookout for the Lollipop Person who has an alarming tendency to leap out from nowhere. The Volvo Driver would also be advised to try and understand the mindset of the Lollipop Person and what makes her / him tick.

So, who is a Lollipop Person? Usually, they are retired gentlefolk with one foot in the grave and the other one on a banana skin. Realisation of this terminal condition does nothing for their general demeanour and they regard it as their mission in life to take it out on the motorist - *any* motorist. They are often pensioned-off tax inspectors or failed traffic wardens with attitude, which should give you some idea of their mentality. Now add the obligatory peaked cap, a fluorescent yellow plastic uniform and a huge "STOP CHILDREN" sign, and give them the absolute power to stop the Volvo Driver dead in his tracks at any time she / he chooses, as often as she / he chooses, and you begin to see what you're up against. So at this point it would be a good idea to list a few basic characteristics of the Lollipop Person in order to gain a deeper appreciation of the problem:

- They have total power over traffic, are **never** in the wrong, and their enthusiasm for disrupting traffic knows no bounds.

- They never position themselves at pelican or zebra crossings. Anywhere is fair game but they will always choose the most awkward locations in which to leap out and terrorise the traffic.

- They apparently never need to take eyesight tests which you would have thought would have been a priority since sight is one of the first sensory functions to deteriorate with age. You could therefore be forgiven for thinking that the average Lollipop Person probably can't even see the traffic half of the time. Should you encounter one with glaucoma or cataracts then all hell could break loose.

- They will always wait at the side of the road while there's little or no traffic. As soon as she / he sees you coming she / he will leap out and plonk down their lollipop, causing you to slam on your brakes and passers-by to look at you disapprovingly.

- She / he will then glare at you for having the temerity to actually be on the road in the first place. This is rapidly followed by a smug grin.

- When eight or nine schoolchildren need to cross the road she / he will not wait until all the children are assembled. She / he will leap out eight or nine separate times in succession with a single child on each occasion while you sit impotently in an ever-lengthening queue of traffic.

- The number of times she / he does this is inversely proportional to the hurry you're in.

There really is nothing you can do to combat this. The only comfort you can take is from knowing that the Lollipop Person has to be out in all weathers, with the cold, the drizzle and the damp playing merry hell with their arthritis, aggravating their bronchial complaints and generally helping them on their way to the great crossing patrols in the sky.

18.12 Traffic Lights & Warning Lights - These appear in quite a few forms. Let's look at the main ones and see how the Volvo Driver should deal with them:

1. *Ordinary Traffic Lights* - remember the colours of traffic lights, their sequence and what they mean. Green means "go", amber means "caution", and red means "stop". However the Volvo Driver should interpret these as follows to ensure minimal disruption to his schedule:

→ **green:**   Go, go, go - before the lights change to amber.

➔ **amber:**	Go, go, go - before the lights change to red.
➔ **red:**	Go, stand on brakes, stop - you saw the cameras just in time.
➔ **red plus flash:**	You didn't see the cameras just in time.
➔ **red:**	In pole position, ready to beat the car in the inside lane off the mark.
➔ **red & amber:**	Go, go, go.
➔ **green:**	Who cares? You will have gone by then.

2. *Filter Lights* - some traffic lights have a green filter arrow pointing to the left or right at junctions, usually where there's heavy traffic. For example, if you want to turn right you will need to get into the outside lane to await the filter arrow. Of course, you can also use this as a fast lane to go straight on but be prepared for resistance from motorists in the inside lane who mistakenly believe that they have the right of way. This will be after you have held up the entire outside lane for the duration of the filter arrow, to the annoyance of those impatient motorists behind you. *(See also section 18.8 on "Turning Right")*.

3. *Lane Control Signals* - these are used on overhead gantries to denote changing rights of way on multi-lane roads without a central reservation. They can be switched back and forth to ease traffic flow at peak periods, or at least that's the general idea. When encountering this type of system the chances are that you will be heavily outnumbered. You would

112

therefore be advised to actually keep your Volvo in the proper lanes which are denoted by a green downwards pointing arrow. Trying to travel in the lanes marked with a red "X" should only be considered provided you're not **too** far from the nearest Accident & Emergency Department.

4.   *Red Flashing Warning Lights* - these are displayed as two red lights, set to flash alternately, mounted on a high rectangular board. They are used to warn motorists of imminent dangers and once activated you are required to stop immediately and stay stopped until the lights are switched off again. The Volvo Driver is no exception to this rule and any attempt to run the lights will almost certainly be met with dire consequences even before Mr Plod has the chance to feel his collar. After all, consider the reasons for these flashing red lights. They will be found at the following locations:

• at railway level crossings - section 18.17 may shed some light on what is likely to be the outcome of disputing the right of way with the London to Glasgow express.

• at fire and ambulance stations - to give fire and ambulance crews the space to respond quickly to emergency calls. As they leave the station on two wheels they do not want to find that they have to negotiate you in your Volvo stranded smack in the middle of the no-go area like a rabbit caught in headlights.

• at airfields - where the end of the runway backs onto the road and the runway approach lights are on the other side. Strong as the body cage is on your Volvo you may feel a slight bit of "give" in the roof when raked by the wheels of a Tristar.

- at swing bridges or raised bridges - trying to beat a bridge before it's fully raised is a mug's game.

5. *Blue Flashing Warning Lights* - not traffic lights as such but are still of vital importance to the Volvo Driver. These lights are to be found on the roof of Mr Plod's jam sandwich, and also on either side of his radiator badge on the front grille. Mr Plod will activate these lights, possibly together with his sirens, for the following reasons:

- He has reason to believe that you have committed a traffic misdemeanour and would like you to stop so that he can discuss it with you.

- He's in a tearing hurry to get past you and will do so knowing fine well that, unlike you, he has Crown Immunity from prosecution for speeding. His reasons could be:

    - he has actually been directed to a crime scene;

    - he's seen somebody scratching his ear while driving and he's given chase;

    - he's speed testing his new jam sandwich and wants to show everybody else on the road how fast he can go;

    - he's late for his lunch;

    - he's on a promise with WPC Plod (see later);

    - his bladder is about to burst;

    - a combination of any of the above.

(See also section 23 on the Volvo Driver and Mr Plod).

6. *Temporary Traffic Lights* - these are portable traffic light systems which appear as if by magic to control the traffic flow around Road Works or temporary obstructions in the road. Just to make certain that they're taken seriously they usually come equipped with their own portable traffic cameras as well. There are four main principles associated with temporary traffic lights which the Volvo Driver would do well to remember. These principles are derived from Sod's Law and are as follows:

- Temporary traffic lights will be erected for the smallest obstacle which could be safely negotiated by the traffic in both directions if the lights weren't there in the first place.

- These lights will always be at green. They will only change to red as you approach them and absolutely nothing comes through from the opposite direction while you wait.

- While waiting at temporary traffic lights for an eternity you decide that they have stuck on red. As you proceed regardless you will then meet the one other vehicle coming in the opposite direction - at the narrowest part of the road works.

- This other vehicle will be a jam sandwich.

18.13 Reversing - Apart from the natural manoeuvres associated with parking *(see section 21)* there will be many occasions when the Volvo Driver will need to reverse his car. This may or may not be associated with the "3-point turn" manoeuvre that you will have practised to perfection for your driving test and have never used since. You may have to reverse your Volvo for many reasons to ensure timely continuity of your journey, and the following are prime examples that spring to mind:

1.   *Reversing back up motorway slip roads* - this is especially important when, not previously having been able to assess traffic conditions on the motorway you want to join, you start down the slip road only to see that you're about to join a 10-mile gridlock. You would not have seen this until you started down the slip road so you would be justified in taking evasive action and reversing back up it on the hard shoulder. However, this is not to be recommended should you find yourself sharing the slip road with Mr Plod stationed there having his lunch, or on red alert waiting to pounce on unsuspecting motorists on the motorway below.

2.   *Reversing back up one-way streets* - the Volvo Driver will not need reminding that local councils are responsible for some of the biggest hindrances that any driver has to face. There are legions of faceless Town Hall non-entities whose sole mission in life is to dream up new ways of obstructing and inconveniencing the motorist. Traffic "calming" measures such as humps or chicanes are a prime example *(see section 18.15).* Another is the creation of a one-way street where previously negotiable town centres become no-go zones almost overnight by making through roads into pedestrian precincts and all the surrounding roads into one-way streets, all going in different directions. The result is gridlocked chaos and finding yourself driving round three sides of a square to get from A to B when previously it was a 100-yard dash in a straight line. Strange, isn't it, that the goons responsible for these "progressive" traffic measures never seem to live in the towns they affect.

But back to one-way streets. There is no reason at all why the Volvo Driver should not utilise these to his own advantage. If you need to get to the other end of a one-way street, and you're at the wrong end and in the wrong direction, you can still negotiate it. But don't draw unnecessary attention to yourself by trying to drive up it against the flow of traffic. Such blatant disregard for the rules will not be appreciated by the local constabulary. You must be more subtle. First of all, where there is a one-way street there are usually several. Choose the one with the least traffic. Drive past it, stop and gently reverse around the corner and into the street. Then stop and take stock of the situation. To all intents and purposes you will look as though you are parked, and you will certainly be facing the right way. Then gradually work your way up the street, backwards. When you successfully reach the other end you can pretend that you've just driven into it by accident, so switch your hazard warning lights on and reverse back into the road you wanted to be on in the first place. This is when you find that, since you were last there, the road you are in is now part of a bigger one-way system and you are merrily carried along on a tidal wave of traffic in the opposite direction to the way you wanted to go, round and round and straight past the bottom of the road you've just emerged from - where you started your reversing manoeuvres half an hour ago.

3.   *Reversing onto a main road from a driveway* - if you live in a suburban area and on a main road the chances are that your driveway opens straight out onto the road. When you turn into your drive you'll have to go in front first because no vehicle in their right mind is going to stop and twiddle their thumbs while you stop your Volvo and reverse it up your drive, and the incessant traffic means that there will be hardly any gaps for you to exploit. So when you come to drive out again you'll have to do it backwards and reverse out onto the main road. This is going to cause problems - not so much for you but more for the traffic on the main road that's going to have to stop and let you out. And they will stop, because you're driving a Volvo and they will want to pay their due

respects. Well, that's the theory of it, anyway. In reality you will need to be a bit more patient because some of the other drivers just don't appreciate, or care (or both) that you have an important schedule to keep, and you need to be out on that road, pronto. So start to reverse your Volvo down your drive and when you reach the gate switch on your hazard warning lights. This will not only alert the on-coming traffic to your existence but hopefully will deter small boys, old ladies and other pedestrians from trying to walk across the back end of your Volvo as you reverse. At this point, whatever you do, ***don't stop***. Stopping or hesitating will be taken as a sign of weakness by other drivers on the road and your hard-won street cred will go down the tubes. Keep going and gradually ease the rear of your Volvo over the pavement and onto the road, turning your steering wheel in the process to align yourself with the traffic.

Just like when you join a main road from a side road *(sections 18.8.2 and 18.9.1)* you may encounter the odd intolerant driver, and a blast on the horn, flashing of the headlights and impolite gesticulations may ensue as he slams on his brakes. At this point raise your hand in a gesture of thanks, raising the temperature even further, then complete your reversing manoeuvre and speed off, not forgetting to switch off your hazard lights. Though this sounds a fairly straightforward manoeuvre you should always be mindful of the following:

- The vehicle that has given way to you should ideally be smaller than yours.

- The vehicle that has given way to you should ideally ***not*** be a jam sandwich.

- Make sure you close your garage doors after you've backed your Volvo out but ***before*** you start to reverse down the drive. Reversing onto the road, and then having to stop, get out of the car, trot back up the drive to close the garage could result in you having an unscheduled meeting with the driver of the vehicle that's just stopped to let you in. You may then incur further delays as you pick yourself up off the ground and go back indoors to change your suit.

4.   *Emergency turn-arounds* - there will be occasions when an emergency will require you to turn the car round and go back in the opposite direction. An example of this is when you find yourself stuck in a traffic jam at temporary traffic lights and you've just driven past the last escape road. No problem. Just swing your Volvo across the road and back again in a 3, 4 or even a 7-point turn - whatever it takes. Ignore the impatient motorists coming towards you who have just spent the best part of half an hour themselves getting through the lights and expecting a clear road. Ignore them also when, having completed your turn-around and driven off the pavement you now stop to turn right up the escape road and block the entire road system because the traffic in the line you were in can't open up a space for you until the traffic lights change. And they can't move then because the on-coming traffic at the lights is still stationary because they're all jammed up behind you. This phenomenon is known as *instant gridlock* and will not only earn you Volvo Brownie Points but also a mention at the Volvo Owners' Club annual bash.

An Old Wives' Tale - never lose sight of, or fail to appreciate, the change in handling characteristics of your Volvo when you reverse it. In particular, turning the steering wheel as you reverse will result in the front of the car swinging out. This phenomenon is often lost on our lady drivers which the body repair shops of most Volvo garages can bear testimony to. If you think I'm biased I offer you a cautionary story:

Once upon a time a husband and his wife and two friends visited a country restaurant one evening and parked up in the drive alongside an old oak tree. After the meal the wife, being the only sober member of the party, took the car keys to drive home. The car was one of the now-classic Volvo 122S series and was in pristine condition. The wife started the car and started to reverse, turning the steering wheel to get the car out of the space. Now, it was on good authority that this oak tree was planted in the reign of Richard the Lionheart and had minded its own business ever since, surviving storms, plagues, wars, Robin Hood, Dutch Elm Disease, alien visitations and all manner of disasters. And then a weird thing happened which to this day has never been fully explained. As the wife reversed the car suddenly to everybody's horror and without warning the oak tree jumped out, stove in the Volvo's front wing, and then jumped back again, assuming its previous position as if nothing had happened.

I know this to be a true story - it was my Volvo 122S. Touchy things, these oak trees.

18.14   Things you should not do while driving - The Standard Highway Code requires you to have proper control of your vehicle at all times, and quite right too. The *Volvo Drivers' Highway Code* fully endorses these sentiments. You should therefore pay particular attention to the following activities when driving your Volvo:

> 1.   *Using mobile phones* - the curse of modern society. You can't venture out of your house these days without encountering people scurrying around with mobile phones clamped to their ears. Or take a train or bus ride without having to listen to somebody else's totally fatuous conversation conducted in a loud voice for the general benefit of all in the vicinity. Mobile phone calls should, as a matter of courtesy to other people, be conducted with a degree of privacy, and where better to do this than in the comfort of your Volvo.

However, using a mobile phone while actually driving your Volvo can be a dicey business. Don't sit in the fast lane of the M6 at 90 mph trying to dial up your colleagues / secretary / wife / mistress / stress counsellor - use the inside lane where you're less visible. Better still, ensure that you stay within the law by having your Volvo fitted with a hands-free kit that allows you to maintain full control of your car while still being able to chat away, totally oblivious to the speed cameras you're whizzing past.

2.   *Courting* - research has proved conclusively that Volvos make excellent vehicles for courting couples; i.e. plenty of leg room in the front and leg-over room in the back. It goes without saying that any clandestine activities must take place when the car is stationary. Romantic snuggles while driving the car are not recommended, and you must maintain control of your car at all times. Should your companion have to implore you to use both hands then you must refuse - you need at least one for driving.

3.   *Shaving* - no, I'm not joking. Sightings have been reported of drivers actually using battery-operated shavers as they race up the motorway. Naturally, these will not be Volvo Drivers due to their inherent sense of social responsibility and road safety, but it is nevertheless a matter of great concern. If one of these lunatics loses control of their car because of this they could well cause a nasty accident which could damage your Volvo through no fault of your own. You should then insist on prosecuting the offender to the fullest extent of the law in order to preserve the high standards by which the Volvo Driver lives. After all, there are times and places for a lady to

shave her legs and the driving seat of a car at full throttle isn't one of them.

4.   *Eating and drinking* - very similar to using a mobile phone or a shaver. Don't do it - you don't have proper control of your car. If you have to eat, stop at a roadside Greasy Spoon or motorway service station and sample the exotic fare on offer. You can always pull into a lay-by a bit further on to throw up.

The same goes for drinking cans of pop or cups of coffee poured by your passenger. This is OK provided there's somewhere for you to put the can or cup while driving. Volvo's are actually equipped with cup-holders but again this is not a lot of use if you have to brake sharply while trying to drink a scalding hot cup of coffee and the whole lot ends up in your lap. Sunroofs were not designed for you to emerge from them while driving.

5.   *Smoking* - very much like the scalding hot cup of coffee, only worse. A lit cigarette butt, when dropped into the groin, is considerably hotter than a cup of coffee. It's a mini-furnace and scrabbling around at high speeds trying to retrieve it before it gives you a pyro-vasectomy can cause all sorts of problems - for you and everybody else on the road who are wondering what the hell you're up to as you frantically swerve from side to side. The underlying principle here is don't smoke while driving - simple as that. This is apart from the manoeuvres and contortions necessary to get the fag out of the packet, into your mouth and lit in the first place, without driving off the road.

6.   *Changing tapes, CDs etc* - in a practical sense tape and CD players are there for a reason - so that you can listen to tapes and CDs during your journey. However, you're going to be spending some time changing tapes, fast-forwarding, reversing and generally fiddling around which may incur the displeasure of Mr Plod if he happens to drive by and catch

you driving without the requisite two hands on your steering wheel. As before, best to always have a companion with you to act as musical co-ordinator.

7.   *Reading a map* - attempting to read while driving is a sure way to court disaster. And these disasters can range from actually driving off the road while trying to read a creased, upside-down map instead of looking where you're going, to upsetting Mr Plod who has decided to follow you and discover the reason for your erratic driving. There is, however, one sure way to guarantee that the Volvo Driver will throw caution to the winds and that's when a lady passenger is the navigator and therefore the principal map reader. This is when a simple journey becomes a Magical Mystery Tour as she struggles with the intricacies of mysterious coloured lines, map symbols and contours, and a planned trip to Hereford ends up in Hartlepool ("*well, they both begin with 'H', don't they?*"). This can have the following consequences for the Volvo Driver:

- increases the blood pressure.

- reduces the life expectancy of the Volvo Driver / lady map reader relationship.

- confirms the need for a tougher sponsor on his Anger Management Programme.

The best solution to this problem is for the Volvo Driver to memorise the route he needs to take before he sets out - parrot-fashion like an actor reading his lines. Alternatively, invest in a Satellite Navigation System / GPS *(see section 17.9)*.

18.15 Traffic Calming Measures - Like everybody else on the road the Volvo Driver is being subjected to an ever-increasing mass of "traffic calming measures" which are springing up all over the country.

At first sight, this appears to be a perplexing waste of public money. We already have "traffic calming measures" - they're called police cars - and road works - and traffic jams, etc etc. (see next section). But apparently this is not enough and further measures are required to reduce the speed of the Volvo and every other driver in both urban and rural areas. These "traffic calming measures" originate from the Town Hall's "Highways Officers" desperate to justify their existence, and are almost always foisted onto the motorist with little or no demand from the local residents.

There are many types of traffic calming measures, depending upon where you live, and the imaginative powers of the Highways Officers responsible for dreaming them up and authorising them. So let's see what sort of speed-reducing obstacles you may encounter in your Volvo as you attempt to race through the streets of say, London, Newcastle, or any other town or city for that matter. Traffic calming measures are classed as man-made and natural (or man un-made):

Man-made Traffic Calming Measures:

1.   *Speed Humps* - great convex mounds of concrete extending across the full width of the road designed to slow you down and leave parts of your car all over the road if you take them too fast. There are, however, other side effects of the speed hump which the Highways Officers choose to ignore:

- Speed humps also slow down the emergency services. They can also offer a robust challenge to the paramedic who is busy trying to insert a drip into a seriously ill patient with the ambulance bouncing up and down like a fairground ride.

- Air quality in the vicinity of speed humps takes a nosedive as drivers continuously brake and then rev up again as they negotiate the humps.

2.   *Chicanes* - great big alternating peninsulas of kerbed concrete stuck out in the street which has the immediate effect of slowing anything down, Volvos included. You can of course choose to ignore them and just drive over them, particularly with a 4x4, but do give them the once-over first:

- Make sure there are no nasty posts stuck at the end of the peninsulas for you to wrap yourself around.

- As for mini-roundabouts *(see section 18.7)* make sure you can drive over them without having to call out the AA for replacement petrol tanks, suspension struts, exhaust systems etc.

3.   *Narrowings* - a bit like chicanes, only the peninsulas of kerbed concrete are directly opposite each other, usually with a large black post stuck on the end of each peninsula for removing your wing mirrors. This creates a bottleneck of around 6'6" available width for you to drive through, assuming of course that your Volvo isn't 6'7" or more wide. With a narrowing at each end of the street this does create a nice peaceful environment for the residents who are effectively sealed off from the noise and nuisance of motorists using the street as a rat-run. They are also effectively sealed off from fire engines, ambulances and other essential services who might want to gain access.

4.   *Kerb Extensions* - a variation on the chicane and narrowing, except that the kerbed peninsulas stick out from only one side of the road. The Highways Officer will obviously have his own reasons for constructing these obstacles, but for the Volvo Driver they provide even more grief in his already hectic day:

- The kerb is often just an extension of the pavement of a side road protruding into a main road. Nobody really knows what this is supposed to achieve, except for making turning from the side road onto the main road a much more hazardous manoeuvre. Let's assume that you want to turn left onto the main road in your Volvo. Having performed the preliminary manoeuvres *(see section 18.9)* you now find that you have to stick the front of the car out so far across the road to make the turn the traffic in both directions has to stop - if you're lucky, that is. Otherwise you end up playing dodgems with fast-moving traffic determined not to yield an inch.

- Sometimes the kerb protrudes across fully half the width of the road with an alternating peninsula a hundred or so yards away; a sort of stretched-out chicane. The space in between then has traffic in one direction always giving way to the other in a "priority over on-coming traffic" / "give way to on-coming traffic" pantomime. This doesn't calm the traffic so much as stops it dead in its tracks, and certainly does little to calm the Volvo Driver on a tight schedule.

5.   *Cushions* - these are curved sections of raised road surface but they don't extend to the full width of the road like speed humps. They do, in fact, resemble giant concrete cushions, hence the name. However, the Traffic Gestapo have reckoned without the Volvo Driver, or the driver of any car with a wide wheelbase, for that matter. Faced with a cushion the Volvo Driver can give the obstacle a quick visual once-over to make sure the height is OK, then just line up the Volvo's wheelbase with the cushion and drive straight over it. Thereafter, as all cushions are essentially the same, you can proceed unhindered at your chosen speed. Having effectively

neutralised the cushion as a traffic-calming measure the Highways Officer will then have the task of explaining away another £3 million road scheme failure.

6.   *Tables* - this is where sections of the road are elevated to the level of the pavement. These elevated sections extend across the width of the road and are usually found at junctions with side roads. So the Volvo Driver hits a ramp to go up, drives straight across the elevated "table" section, and down off the ramp at the other end. Since the actual boundaries between road and pavement are now somewhat blurred you will find that, rather than by improving safety by reducing traffic speed it actually worsens it by making it a lot easier to drive on the pavement - an opportunity not lost on our cyclist friends *(see section 3)*. It also makes it a lot easier for confused or elderly pedestrians to wander into the elevated road section without realising it. Another triumph for Town Hall innovative thinking.

7.   *Multi-mini-roundabouts* - see section 18.7.

Natural Traffic Calming Measures:

These consist of the great potholes in the road that the local council can't afford to fix because they've spent all their budget on building chicanes, humps, tables, cushions and mini-roundabouts. And when they do get round to filling them in any old gravel, mixed with crisp packets, beer cans and bike frames will do. This work will be carried out completely independently of the gas company, phone company, water company etc who will then arrive on the scene, totally independent of each other, and promptly dig it all up again *(see section 22 on Road Works)*.

18.16 Congested Roads & Traffic Jams - Following the section on traffic calming measures it seems only natural to address the biggest traffic calming measure of them all - the ever-present congested road which leads to the traffic jam which in turn leads to total gridlock. Let's face it, as a traffic calming measure the gridlock is singularly the most effective strategy known to man. However, it's only the vehicles that are calmed. The effect upon their drivers is exactly the opposite.

Congested roads, traffic jams and gridlocks know no social boundaries and they can be found bringing whole stretches of motorways to a halt as easily as they can in towns and city centres. In fact some of Europe's biggest car parks can be found between junctions 22 and 29 of the M1, and on the whole of the M25. A momentary lapse of concentration or an inadvertent wrong turn can find the Volvo Driver ensnared in a nightmare of stationary traffic from which there is no escape. And once trapped the Volvo Driver can then find himself subjected to further indignities and inconveniences; for example:

- Rolling to a final halt in a box junction that has a spy camera hovering overhead.

- Hearing a DJ on the local radio telling motorists to avoid the very traffic jam you've just got stuck in.

- Forgetting to bring a packed lunch with you.

- Finding yourself stuck in an area where you can't get a signal on your mobile to advise your 11.00 am appointment that you're going to be late.

- On a dual carriageway or motorway, finding yourself stuck in the one lane that's not moving at all. When you do manage to switch lanes the lane you've just left is now moving faster than yours.

- Your bladder reminding you that the call of nature that you should have answered an hour ago is long overdue.

For the Volvo Driver to try and avoid these situations it is necessary to go back to basics and find out what causes them in the first place. Local councils will have you believe that the causes remain obscure, and have deep underlying sociological implications because then they can claim they can't do anything about it. In the real world, however, the reasons for gridlocked roads are much more simple. Try these:

(1)   The roads themselves are dropping to bits, usually through council under-funding, necessitating countless road works complete with contraflows to bring the traffic to a standstill.

(2)   There is actually more traffic using these roads, aggravating the problem still further. This additional traffic is derived from two sources; firstly, more people now have cars. Secondly, lousy public transport means that more people take to their cars.

(3)   An existing dual carriageway being converted into a single-lane road with a bus lane.

(4)   Back-street rat-runs to avoid the congestion on the main roads now have speed humps, chicanes and narrowings etc.

(5)   Any combination of all the previous four reasons.

So, what can be done to make life easier for the Volvo Driver? Well, there have been many ideas put forward as to how congestion should be tackled but none are quite as innovative as the *Congestion Charge* dreamed up by the powers-that-be in our capital city. Quite simply, this entails charging motorists a tax to drive in Central London to try and reduce the number of vehicles jamming up the city. The Volvo Driver would be justified in detecting a certain irony in this since it is the same powers-that-be that have created a lot of the congestion problems in the first place by introducing bus and cycle lanes, speed humps, one-way streets, traffic lights programmed to change every five seconds and generally failing to provide an adequate public transport system as a viable alternative to using a car. In fact there are rumours that the Mayoral Office actually believes that people *like* driving in London. It has obviously not occurred to these poor deluded souls that most people have no choice and if London had a public transport system that actually worked you wouldn't see a Volvo within 50 miles of the place.

18.17 Railway Level Crossings - Unfortunately, this is another of those very rare occasions when it is advisable for the Volvo Driver to know his limitations and acknowledge that there are some obstacles which even he can't overcome. At some point in your journey you may encounter the one feature in the British road system that is guaranteed to stop you dead in your tracks, whether you like it or not - the railway level crossing. It is a fundamental law of nature that when road meets railway the train has right of way and it would be foolhardy, to say the least, to challenge this in a practical situation. Remember section 9 on trams? Well now think bigger, heavier, and much, much faster.

Level crossings are of three types; those with automatic barriers, those with manually operated barriers, and those with no barriers at all. Let's look at each in turn:

> 1.   *Level crossings with automatic barriers* - these level crossings always give you adequate warning before closing. Before the barriers come down there are flashing red lights and a warning bell. You will need to stop at these and wait for the barriers to drop, to be followed eventually by the train. In fact, you may as well switch off the engine and wander over to Joe's café for a bacon butty and a cup of tea. It's well

documented that our railways are probably the worst-run in the western world, with punctuality a national joke. Add to this the fact that the Health & Safety Gestapo insist on setting level crossing barriers to close when the train is still ten miles away, just to be on the safe side, and you will find you've got a good quarter of an hour before the train actually arrives. And when you're really pushed for time there will be a train coming the other way as well, timed to arrive fifteen minutes after the first one. At this point you would be advised to accept that the gods have got it in for you, and keep calm. This is particularly important where the barriers are of the type that only come down across half the width of the road on each side, therefore offering the temptation to use them as a chicane and chance beating the train to it. If you try it the Law of Sod has decreed that you will do so on the one occasion when the train is on time.

Now, Volvo's *SIPS* systems are legendary but they have been designed to protect the occupants of your Volvo from side impacts with road vehicles, not the *Flying Scotsman*. It is therefore inadvisable, when at a level crossing, to dispute the right of way with an inter-city express. At best, you will see your beautiful Volvo reduced to kitchen foil in the bat of an eyelid; at worst you will end up qualifying for a pair of wings, a halo and a white nightie as the newest member of the celestial Volvo Owner's Club.

2.   *Level crossings with manually operated barriers* - these are the old-fashioned type and some are still in use today. Instead of barriers which are automatically triggered by a train a signalman or other railway operative is notified of an approaching train and plods out to manually close the crossing gates. These level crossings will, however, be fitted with the red flashing warning lights (usually). In many ways they are a lot safer than the automatic type since they *are* proper gates, and dogs,

small boys and cyclists can't duck under them or go around them. The downside of this is the time at which these gates are closed prior to the train arriving is indirectly proportional to how late you already are, but directly proportional to the railway operative's frame of mind and the degree of arthritis in his joints. So the Volvo Driver may actually find himself being held up for longer than he would have done at a crossing with automatic barriers.

3.   *Level crossings with no barriers (Railway Telephones)* - these are just simple crossings of road and railway tracks with no barriers at all, and gives the Volvo Driver complete control over his destiny. The crossing barriers have been replaced with a Railway Telephone and it's up to the Volvo Driver to stop before crossing the tracks and ring somebody up. If you're lucky a disembodied voice, usually pre-recorded, will tell you whether a train is on its way or whether it's safe to cross. Because of the basic nature of this type of level crossing you only ever find them on railway lines that are hardly used, or even mothballed, and where the likelihood of an accident is virtually zero. However, do bear the following in mind:

- The line may look decrepit, with rusty tracks and grass growing up between the sleepers, but don't take it for granted. It's not unknown for the railway companies, particularly at weekends when there is "essential maintenance" to be done on the main line, to divert trains down these near-mothballed tracks to deliver a rude awakening to the complacent Volvo Driver. The golden rule is that if there is a modern-looking level crossing sign and / or a Railway Telephone to give the impression that the line is occasionally in use, then it probably is.

- Because the line is hardly used it's a pretty safe bet that the Railway Telephone doesn't work, either. This may not be immediately apparent as you struggle to make contact with Mission Control at the other end of the clapped-out phone. Just make sure that you haven't inadvertently parked your Volvo across the railway tracks while you're making the call.

18.18 River Crossings - Your journey can take you through a wide range of scenery and geographical features. At some point you may find yourself having to cross a stretch of water, which can vary from a small stream to a mile-wide river estuary. So the size of the water feature in question is largely going to dictate the method you use to get from one side to the other. You basically have four options when faced with water; you can go through it, over it, across it or under it, by ford, bridge, ferry or tunnel respectively. Each offers its own unique challenge to the Volvo Driver as we can see:

1.   *Fords and Floods* - in the same way as you find railway tracks crossing your road at level crossings you can often find a flow of water crossing your road. These aquatic crossing points are called *fords* and can be particularly noticeable after heavy rainfall. A ford is intended to be navigable by vehicles and they will be of two types:

(1)   A small stream issuing from a culvert at road level where the water flows across the road and into a stream on the other side. Normally, the depth of water is just a few inches.

(2)   The more adventurous type of ford which crosses a river. The crossing point is at the shallowest part of the river and consists of a causeway which is usually permanently submerged a foot or so under the surface of the water.

Under normal circumstances (i.e. excluding flash floods) you could safely navigate your way across a ford. However, if you are faced with a river ford as described in (2) above it is strongly recommended that you stop and give it the once-over first:

- Have a good look at the **depth** of the water. Amphibious cars are only found in James Bond movies and although you may consider your Volvo to be an all-weather car you may detect some loss of performance when submerged under four feet of water.

- Have a good look at the **flow** of the water. You may be a Volvo Driver but you are not Moses. Driving into a deep ford and expecting the waters to part miraculously to smooth your passage across could result in deep disappointment, to say nothing of the recovery costs of salvaging your Volvo from a quarter of a mile downstream, and the stiff upper lip you will need to maintain in the face of a crowd of locals howling with laughter.

2.   *Bridges* - there are many types but they all fall into two basic categories; those that split the road by raising themselves up or swinging themselves around to permit the passage of a boat, and those that don't:

(1)   *Swing Bridges and Raised Bridges* - this is where your road suddenly disappears for a finite period of time. As you approach a bridge that's about to be raised or swung open you will be greeted by a set of red flashing warning lights *(see section 18.12)*. You will be required to stop at these lights and wait. This will be a bit like waiting for railway crossings *(section 18.17)* when you had time for a cuppa and a sandwich before the gates open again. However, at these bridges you'll have time

for a three course meal and a quick browse round the local shopping mall before the bridge closes and you can be on your way. Fortunately, these types of bridges are very few and far between.

(2)   *Static Bridges* - these are the normal types of bridge that don't open and close, and range from the humble hump-back bridge across a stream to the mighty suspension bridge crossing river estuaries. Each has its own unique characteristics. The hump-back bridge is designed to be a Volvo launch pad if you take it too fast, and the suspension bridge can carry several lanes of traffic but at a cost *(see section 18.20 on Toll Roads)*.

3.   *Ferries* -   there are still a few car ferries around which the Volvo Driver can use for crossing rivers and other stretches of water. Ferries are great social levellers. It doesn't matter what type of vehicle you drive, or how fast it goes, once on the ferry you switch off the engine and let the ship take the strain. This does not, of course, prevent the Volvo Driver from wangling his way to pole position on the dock to ensure that he can get on board the ferry first. However, if the same ramp is used for unloading the ferry this will mean that he will then be last off. Some you win; some you lose.

4.   *Tunnels* - these are covered in more detail in the next section, 18.19.

18.19 Road Tunnels - You may, during the course of your journey, be faced with a road tunnel. Popular on the more mountainous continent the UK only has a few of these to worry about, and most of these can be found under river estuaries (Tyne, Mersey, Thames). You will find the odd one hacked into the countryside and at airport terminals (Leeds, Heathrow) but generally road tunnels are not widespread. This is just as well for the Volvo Driver since tunnels are not exactly designed to speed the flow of traffic:

- They are almost always single lane with a double white line down the middle, putting any thoughts of overtaking totally out of the question.

- They have very low speed limits which are often enforced by an official-looking jeep armed with a flashing blue light on a pole. This jeep spends its time driving in front of a queue of traffic that's already spent a half-hour queueing at the toll plaza, and heading a convoy through the tunnel at a nice safe 20 mph.

- They have totally inadequate ventilation systems. This only becomes apparent as you sit in the jeep-led convoy, breathing in an invigorating blend of carbon monoxide and diesel fumes. The internal air circulation system inside your Volvo for once works against you as all it does is pump the noxious mixture round the cabin that bit faster.

- To their credit most tunnels are lit so at least you will be able to see what you're doing when the time comes to change your flat tyre. This contrasts sharply with road tunnels in Norway, for example, where they can be eight miles long with no lighting.

The road tunnel provides yet another opportunity for the Volvo Driver to demonstrate his qualities. You can't avoid them (the alternative is usually a 40-mile round trip), so you may as well go with the flow. Anyway, the sight of a Volvo Driver displaying calm, patience and courtesy is a salutary lesson to other road users, even if such a sighting does happen slightly less frequently than Halley's Comet.

18.20   Pay-as-you-go (Toll Roads etc) - In common with all other road users above the level of cyclist the Volvo driver pays handsomely through his taxes for the privilege of using his road. Just consider - you pay Road Fund Licence (car tax) to get your Volvo on the road in the first place; you pay extortionate excise duty on each litre of fuel you buy; then you pay parking charges when you actually want to stop the car. If that's not enough, and you are unfortunate enough to live or work in central London, then you'll also get clobbered for the privilege of driving in that fair city by Mr Livingstone's Congestion Charge. This is without any additional costs that you may incur through fines as a result of falling foul of Mr Plod's speed cameras.

Now the Volvo Driver may just consider this expense to be justified if the road system he uses is efficient, effective and of reasonable quality, but it isn't. Far from it. Our roads are congested, under-funded and falling to bits. Road Works litter the network and the Volvo Driver is faced with interminable delays to every journey. To address this, one of the solutions that the Highways Departments have come up with is to build new roads and short cuts in the form of tunnels and bridges which offer a faster journey time. Now you may think that these new roads, tunnels and bridges would be adequately funded from your taxes and again you would be wrong. Never passing up a golden opportunity to milk the motorist the Highways Departments align themselves with market forces and charge extra taxes, in the form of tolls, for the convenience of using these new thoroughfares. They justify this as "maintenance costs".

Being a Volvo Driver your knee-jerk reaction to this is to take great exception to this additional assault on your finances but unfortunately there's not an awful lot you can do if you want to use these toll roads, tunnels and bridges since the toll money is collected at a series of booths stretched across the road. This is called a *toll plaza* and there's no legal way around it. But you can register your protest. When arriving at a toll plaza you will notice that at least half of the booths are closed, delaying your journey still further. The booths that are open have a green traffic light above them, and each has its own little red and green traffic light system for "stop" and "go" and sometimes a little barrier. The booths can be manned or unmanned and the frame of mind that you find yourself in at the time will dictate which type you're going to use. Then proceed as follows, reasoning that as you're late anyway a few more minutes won't make a lot of difference:

1.   *Manned Toll Booths* - these should be approached as follows:

    • for the average toll of 50p to £1.50 always offer the booth attendant the highest denomination of banknote. In fact, if you can, keep one or two with you for this specific purpose. A £50 note is favourite. Refuse to accept the attendant's protests *("I can't change that, mate")* using the argument that the banknote only represents the money taken for the last 30 or 40 vehicles so he can change it. It is legal tender. He now has two choices; either change it gracelessly and let you through, or keep you at the booth. In the latter case, switch off the engine, park up and proceed to read the newspaper bought specially for this purpose. As the traffic builds up behind you get out of the car and make sure everybody knows it's not your fault. If he then shuts the booth down drive off regardless, safe in the knowledge that the CCTV cameras will have clearly shown your willingness to pay, and his resulting intransigence. You will need this evidence once Mr Plod of the Tunnel Police catches up with you.

    • If the attendant does change the note for you, ask for a VAT receipt.

2.   *Unmanned Toll Booths* - you're only supposed to head for these if you've got the right money for the toll. Paying the toll just entails chucking the right amount of coins into a collecting basket whereupon, presumably, the money is automatically weighed and compared to calibrated standards.

This changes the red traffic light to green to allow you to proceed. Faced with one of these you will need to do the exact opposite of what you did for manned toll booths and select the *lowest* value coins for your toll; preferably 1p and 2p pieces. Keep a stock of these in the car. As the "calibrated" collecting baskets enjoy a reputation for wide inaccuracy much fun can be had when you come to pay your toll. You can either chuck in the whole lot in one go and wait for it to blow a fuse, or lump it in coin by coin. Either way, it's a better than even chance that it won't register which will set off all sorts of alarms and flashing lights. It has been reported that the introduction of several metal washers into the mix of coins can further enhance the entertainment value but the Volvo Driver should rise above such deceptions. After all, once you've activated the alarms, there is a highly probable chance of being pulled over by Mr Plod and you'll need to prove you're squeaky-clean.

19.   DRIVING ON MOTORWAYS:

And now we come to the pièce de resistance - the real, and I mean *real*, reason why Volvos are built and why their drivers like to drive them - to drive on motorways. The motorway is home territory for the Volvo in much the same way as Silverstone is for Formula 1 cars. It is their domain.

First of all, let's define what we mean by "motorways". These are the proper three or four lane highways and not the pretend versions; dual carriageways with hard shoulders such as the Doncaster by-pass which masquerade as motorways. There is an etiquette for motorway driving for the *Volvo Drivers' Highway Code* which we can now summarise:

19.1   Lane Allocation - This is very simple:

- *Inside (slow) lane* - for trucks, lorries, coaches, abnormal loads and geriatrics in 10-year old Micras who really have no business being on a motorway.

- *Middle lane* - for other cars and naughty trucks who decide to overtake other trucks that are in the inside lane, thereby forcing everybody else into the outside (fast / Volvo) lane.

- *Outside (fast) lane* - should be for Volvos, but will also include flashy cars such as Mercs, Jags and BMWs. Unfortunately the fast lane is also used by jam sandwiches and unmarked police cars, the Company Rep, Boy Racer and the stragglers forced over by the overtaking trucks in the middle lane (see above).

- *Hard shoulder* - for broken-down vehicles, cars containing vomiting children, and motorists stopped by jam sandwiches adding to their quota for the day. It must be stressed that the hard shoulder is definitely ***not*** to be used for:

  -        Parking up to admire the scenery;

  -        A pit stop to answer a call of nature;

  -        Roadside picnicking;

  -        A crafty "undertake" of mobile cranes etc ambling along on the inside lane.

19.2   Lane Discipline - For 3-lane motorways the Volvo Driver should observe the following rules:

- All cars, trucks, lorries, buses and coaches should keep to the inside lane except when overtaking. This does not apply to

Volvo Drivers who will already be in the outside lane.

- The middle lane is for overtaking the slower vehicles in the inside lane. This does not apply to Volvo Drivers who will already be in the outside lane.

- The outside lane is for Volvos, but can unfortunately also include other road users as we've seen in the previous section. Theoretically the outside lane is for overtaking only but human nature being what it is it does tend to become a third cruising lane. I mean, what's the point of pulling over into an outer lane to overtake a slower moving vehicle in your Volvo and then having to pull back again when you know you will have to go through the same routine again a couple of miles further on? Might as well stay where you are.

- Remember the fundamental laws of overtaking that we discussed in section 18.5 and ensure that, as an accomplished Volvo Driver, you abide by them.

19.3   Driving Rules - There are a few fundamental Driving Rules for motorways, many of which we have already covered elsewhere in this book, but we feel that it is important to summarise and emphasise them again at this point. They are as follows:

Rule 1:   Don't drive too close to the vehicle in front in case you have to do an emergency stop. Your Volvo is fitted with superior brakes but the 10-year old banger driven by the plonker behind you almost certainly won't be. And extricating plonkers from the tail end of your Volvo is not only costly but downright inconvenient.

Rule 2:   Conversely, don't leave too much of a gap between you and the car in front. This will only encourage the plonker to overtake (or undertake) and jump into the gap, and you're back to square one.

Rule 3: Set your nearside wing mirror to spot jam sandwiches sneakily heading down slip roads to join the motorway for a spot of speed control fun with the traffic.

Rule 4: On joining a motorway head straight for the outside lane and stay there.

Rule 5: Never be afraid to use your horn to constantly remind other drivers of your presence. Creating a sense of awareness significantly contributes to road safety.

Rule 6: Use your headlight flashers to warn other drivers of your intention to overtake and consequently of the need for them to move out of your way. Now.

Rule 7: Never signal if you intend to pull out into a faster lane. The vehicle behind you will realise that you are driving a Volvo so he (or she) will understand and therefore be expecting it.

Rule 8: Ignore any flashing yellow or amber lights associated with abnormal loads, mobile cranes etc. Do not ignore flashing blue ones.

19.4 Lights & Signals - Motorways have a variety of lighting systems for alerting the Volvo driver to possible hazards ahead, and the appropriate action to be taken. The following types of lighting systems can be found:

● Overhead gantries displaying red flashing lights and a mysterious sequence of arrows. The red lights are intended as a warning and the side-pointing or downward-pointing arrows are informing you that you should either change lanes as soon as it is safe to do so, or leave the motorway altogether at the next exit. You should heed these warnings and obey the signs, if only to avoid the inevitable police road block that lies in wait for those motorists who choose to carry on regardless.

- These overhead gantries can, through the wonders of modern technology, also act as message boards. So instead of warning lights overhead you may suddenly find yourself faced with "40 mph" or "50 mph" or some similar message appropriate to the lane you happen to be in at the time. Sometimes these messages can be really useful, such as "queues ahead", "lane closed ahead" or "accident at next junction" etc, but these will only ever be switched on just after the last exit before the traffic jam starts. As you come to a halt at the gridlock your temper faces fresh challenges as:

  - you hear the road report on your car radio warning you of the hold-up and advising you to leave the motorway at the exit you've just passed;

  - the distracted plonker behind you slams into your rear end because he (or she) has been trying to read all the signs on the gantry instead of looking where he (or she) is going.

- Then we have those square electronic indicator boards which are situated at regular intervals on the central reservation, showing "50" or "40" or some other temporary speed limit. This will guarantee three things:

  (1) These signs always appear on clear roads in near-perfect driving conditions;

  (2) You will drive for miles without seeing any conceivable reason for this temporary speed limit; no accident, no lorry shedding its load, no alien spacecraft - absolutely nothing. Then the next sign says "End".

(3)   As a result of this nobody is taking a blind bit of notice.

Now this means one of two things:

Either - after an accident three months ago somebody has forgotten to switch the damned things off;

Or (more likely) - the police, safe in the assumption that nobody will take a blind bit of notice, have deliberately switched them on to create a "catch patch" complete with the latest digital camera technology. This of course serves no purpose other than ensuring they meet their allocated daily quotas of motorists nicked for speeding.

● Going back to the message boards, overhead gantries are not the only place on the motorway where these can be found. As if the Volvo Driver didn't have enough distractions the Highways Agency has taken to erecting huge electronic message screens along the *side* of the motorway. These screens are used to nag and nanny the Volvo Driver rather than to warn of dangers or hazards ahead. Sometimes, just sometimes, they serve a useful purpose such as warning against tailgating but these tend to be the exception rather than the rule. Most of the messages that flash up defy belief. The following are genuine examples of messages seen on screens alongside British motorways:

(1)   Warnings of the dire consequences of travelling at 71 mph. *(I kid you not, "71 mph" was the actual speed shown)*.

(2)   Statements insisting that there is no difference between a speeding driver and a driver who has been drinking *(Er, just run that past me again?)*.

(3)   Invitations to shop motorists who you consider are speeding, or getting up your nose in some other way. And they provide a telephone number to ring, too. Presumably, if someone is then seen dialling this number on a mobile as they race up the motorway they can be grassed up as well. The possibilities are endless.

As the Volvo Driver is expected to set an example you will be required to take all this in as you drive along. If you do manage to avoid crashing in the process you could test out this hotline phone number. Be aware, though, that mischief is never far away and perish the thought that you would turn off the motorway, pull over and report:

- the registration number of the last jam sandwich that flashed past you;

or

- a fleet of flying saucers preparing to land.

Just remember to block your own phone number to outgoing calls first. Identifying yourself to the authorities through your mobile number is a mug's game.

20.   DRIVING IN ADVERSE WEATHER CONDITIONS:

20.1   Rain - We've covered the essential principles and skills involved here in the section on trucks and lorries *(the Mobile Car Wash - section 11.2)* but we think it essential at this point to look at it again in more detail in view of the potential hazards involved in driving on a wet road. Let's examine the general principles and how the Volvo Driver should tackle them. Rain and wet roads can generate a variety of hazards for the Volvo Driver to face, depending upon whether it's actually raining, or not:

1.   *Wet roads - still raining* - you know that, because the tyres on your Volvo cost upwards of £150 each, they are the best that money can buy. Therefore you are entitled to feel that a wet road in driving rain with two inches of surface water is just as safe as a dry road on a summers day to a Volvo. There is therefore no need to vary your driving in any way. Maintain your speed on the outside lane and carry on regardless, assuming that your windscreen wipers are effective enough to actually allow you to see through the windscreen. This is known as positive driving, and is a triumph of mind over matter. Maintain this philosophy as you turn off motorway at the next exit slip road. At the bottom of the slip road is a roundabout. To negotiate this turn your steering wheel to the left at the same time applying the brakes as you would on a dry road.

It is at this point that you will begin to wonder why, with your wheels locked to the left, you are still going straight on. This is known as **aquaplaning**, and it takes a very skilful Volvo Driver to accomplish this manoeuvre properly. As you pick your way out of the rhododendrons on the roundabout you will ultimately find that insurance companies recognise this skill, which will be reflected in your next insurance premium renewal.

2.   *Wet roads - light drizzle / no rain at all* - probably some of the worst driving conditions can be found on wet roads when it's stopped raining or there is a light drizzle. Not only can a low sun reflect the glare like a mirror, but there will be enough water on the road to ensure that the lorry in front can chuck up all sorts of muck all over your Volvo without the benefit of heavy rain to wash it off. And of course there always

146

will be a lorry in front of you and it won't have any mudflaps. You will need to get past him, and quickly, so you will need to simulate an emergency situation. Once you get the chance to overtake, as you draw level with him, set up a vigorous flashing of lights, toot your horn and point to his nearside, drawing your finger across your throat as you do it. This will encourage him to him to stop quickly and wonder what all the fuss was about. You will then drive on until you realise that your windscreen washers have run out of water and you need to re-fill. Then you find that the garage that you choose to stop at will be same one as the truck that you carved up earlier chooses to stop at to fill up with diesel.

20.2   Ice and Snow - "Ice and snow" - three words guaranteed to strike terror into the hearts of the average British motorist, but not to the Volvo Driver who is made of sterner stuff. "Ice and snow" - the Volvo Driver positively rises to the challenge. After all, haven't Volvos been designed to cope with the worst that the British winter can throw at them? Well, no, actually they haven't. Volvos have been designed to cope with the worst that the **Swedish** winter can throw at them. You know, proper winters with piles of snow, sub-zero temperatures and ice-covered lakes you can drive your Volvo on. Not the damp, miserable apologies that pass for winters here.

Two inches of snow and we grind to a halt, so it becomes very difficult for the Volvo Driver to demonstrate his prowess in snow when all the motorists around him are crawling along like a snail with piles. The Volvo Driver can always get that bit further in snow and reach those parts that other motorists can't reach, which is why the cars stuck the furthest in the snowdrifts on the M74 are usually Volvos.

Icy roads are a danger to any motorist, particularly for those who have not been taught to drive properly in these conditions. Fortunately the Volvo Driver is not subject to such handicaps. He knows his car is made for cold-weather driving and therefore sees little reason to try and compensate for the icy conditions. As we have seen in the previous section the Volvo Driver is able to safely handle wet roads and rainy conditions and ice is, after all, only solid rain. So drive normally. You will find that the roads will be kept clear as the rest of the traffic driving at a more sedate pace scramble to get out of your way, a pirouetting one-and-a-half tonne battering ram. The field or ditch you eventually end up in will make a nice change from all that slippery tarmac.

Note of Caution: You may have realised by now that we haven't mentioned anything about black ice, which presents itself as an invisible sheet of ice on the road. This is deliberate. As you may probably be aware the word "black" is considered "offensive" by the politically correct pigment police that hold sway over our ruling classes. Offensive to them, that is; not the other 99% of the population. However, to ensure that we don't give offence, black ice will henceforth be referred to as *"ice that cannot be seen"*. This will not, of course, make one iota of difference should you hit a patch of it at speed; Volvo or no Volvo, you're history.

20.3   Fog - Driving in fog is a bit like driving in the slipstream of an oil tanker on a wet road as far as visibility goes *(see the Mobile Car Wash, section 11.2)*, except that it's muckier and the visibility is worse. Your techniques for driving in fog should be similar, too. There's little point in trying to use the white lines as guidelines because these white lines have a habit of veering off into side streets. Instead, focus upon the rear lights of the vehicle in front. With respect to *your* lighting systems make sure you have both front and rear foglights switched on. This is especially important when the fog clears. You may blind a few motorists behind you with your rear fogs, but who knows when you may suddenly need them again? No point in wearing out your switches. So focus on the car in front, safe in the knowledge that he will almost certainly be focussing his sights on the car in front of him. Keep in a nice steady convoy, stopping and starting when he stops and starts (for traffic lights etc). If you're all going in roughly the same direction then all will be well. Don't worry if he turns off the highway;

he obviously knows a few local short cuts. Keep behind him and of course he will eventually stop. Stop behind him and stay there until the fog clears. You will then find yourself nicely tucked up behind him on his own driveway at 66 Acacia Avenue while he's wondering who his mysterious visitor is. Well, you can't win them all.

20.4   Wind - With respect to winds the Volvo Driver can encounter two types of wind. That produced *outside* the car by the elements, and that produced *inside* the car by the occupants, the latter usually caused by the individuals concerned consuming large portions of spicy ethnic delicacies the night before. This type of wind is easily dealt with - by turfing the offenders out at the nearest bus stop.

However, winds outside the car usually manifest themselves as side winds, and can be dangerous. At best they can affect your steering and at worst they can blow you and your car across carriageways. Of course, due to the weight and supreme road-holding of the car this will not adversely affect the Volvo Driver. It may, however, affect the car you are overtaking in the inside lane, particularly if it's one of these cheap foreign jobs made out of the type of metal normally found wrapped around a stick of chewing gum. Some of these are so light that they can be blown off course by the slipstream of a passing Volvo. You will need to give these vehicles as wide a berth as possible.

The same thing can happen to "high-siders" such as double-decker buses and furniture vans where the high winds will quite often blow the whole vehicle over. Even your Volvo might get irreparably damaged if one of these decides to roll over and sit on you so, again, give them a wide berth. Caravans are even worse. As we saw in section 6 these are inherently unstable contraptions at the best of times. In high winds they can be positively lethal as they get blown from side to side. Sometimes, if you're very fortunate, they'll get blown off the road altogether, making your journey that much more enjoyable.

20.5   Hot Weather - No, don't laugh. We do occasionally have hot dry days here in the height of summer. The trouble is, that these tend to be the exception rather than the rule so that when it does get a bit on the warm side the great British public tends to go over the top to make the most of it. This can bring its own problems on the roads and fortunately the intensive training that the Volvo Driver undergoes will have prepared him for these eventualities. Also fortunately, the Volvo itself will be equal to the task. So, when faced with a long drive in hot weather, the Volvo Driver will need to be aware of the following, and take appropriate action where required:

- Extreme heat can soften the surface layer of tarmac on the roads. If the weather then reverts to normal and it rains this can turn the road into a skidpan. You should therefore allow sufficient room between you and the vehicle in front to enable you to stop safely should you need to, and also to give yourself that extra bit of space to move into if the car behind can't stop as quickly as you. These principles have been covered in *Rules 1* and *2* in section 19.3 (the section on motorway driving).

- Driving in heat can cause fatigue, so remember to keep the air conditioning on; or if you prefer, the windows and sunroof open. The latter will also enable you to breathe in all that nice fresh carbon monoxide when you get stuck behind a bus in a traffic jam.

- Driving in heat can fray the nerve-ends, particularly when snarled up in a 15-mile tailback resulting in delays to your journey which you feel obliged to make up whenever possible.

However, once delayed you will find that the gods have definitely got it in for you as, thereafter, you find yourself **held up** by a Learner Driver, **wound up** by a Boy Racer, **burned up** by a Company Rep, and finally **pulled up** by a jam sandwich for alleged speeding. This in

150

turn frays the nerve-ends even more, and increases the tendency for road rage, which as we all know is totally out of character for the Volvo Driver. So it's a good job that your training allows you to call upon yet another fundamental law of the Volvo Driver:

"Road rage is for wimps"

(to be repeated through gritted teeth)

21.   PARKING:

Every Volvo Driver will need to park his car once in a while, assuming of course that a suitable space can be found. There are three key issues involved here; where to park , where NOT to park, and how to park. Let's look at each aspect in turn and how the Volvo Driver should approach each one:

21.1   Where to Park - Like all motorists you will, without a shadow of a doubt, be subject to what we now call *Dullroy's Twelve Laws of Parking*. These are as follows:

Law 1:   *There are fewer parking spaces than the number of people wanting to park.*

Law 2:   *Parking spaces are situated as far as possible from the place you actually want to be.*

Law 3:   *The only ticket machines that work will be situated even further away from where you want to be - in the opposite direction.*

Law 4:   *While you are seeking this ticket machine it will be raining - hard.*

Law 5:   *Ticket machines only ever accept the one coin you don't have on you.*

Law 6:   The only available parking spaces are just too narrow for your car.

Law 7:   The only available parking space that fits your car will have a motor-cycle parked smack in the middle of it.

Law 8:   Where there is room for 2 cars to be parallel-parked there will be one car parked symmetrically in the centre, leaving a half-car length at each end.

Law 9:   Maximum parking times will be 15 minutes shorter than the period you want the space for.

Law 10:   Cars causing an obstruction are wheel-clamped to ensure that they stay there.

Law 11:   Where car parks are full, disabled spaces aren't.

Law 12:   Car parks marked on a town plan are at the wrong end of a one-way street which isn't marked as "one way" on the town plan, and you will always approach it from the wrong end.

What makes the Volvo Driver stand out from the rest of the pack is his ability to be that bit smarter, that bit craftier, and that bit more bloody-minded in his interpretation of these Laws than everybody else. No other driving manoeuvre offers the Volvo Driver the opportunity to show his true colours, and you have to remember that as parking spaces are not designed to fit Volvos anyway, you are perfectly entitled to make your own arrangements. The following locations are permissible for parking your Volvo:

   1.   *Short term parking* - this is when you will need to park up for, say, up to 15 minutes:

- Across a line of parked cars in a car park. Use your hazard warning lights to give the trapped motorists the impression that you have only parked for a minute or so.

- On double or single yellow lines. Again, switch on your hazard warning lights to indicate to the traffic warden lurking around the corner watching you that you will only be a moment.

- Across a driveway. However, if the drive is occupied by another Volvo show a bit of respect and park somewhere else.

- At a bus stop. However, should you find yourself sharing the bus stop with a bus that actually wants to use it, a discreet retreat is recommended. Go and find some yellow lines and park on those.

2.   *Long term parking* - this is when you need to park for more than 15 minutes:

- Against a wall in a multi-storey car park, reducing the width available to "through" traffic to just over a car's width.

- In an employee's car park of a large company where access is unhindered by swipe cards and barriers, or a hired jobsworth.

- In a hotel car park "reserved for patrons only". Who's to know?

- In one of those politically-correct "mother and child" parking spaces. After all, you are some mother's child and they don't specify the child's maximum age, do they?

<u>NB:</u> Do **NOT** park in disabled spaces (see next section).

These are just some suggestions. However, should you be unfortunate enough to encounter grief from a hired lackey or the Parking Gestapo, recall to mind another fundamental law of the Volvo Driver:

"Happiness is driving over a traffic warden's foot"

21.2   Where not to Park - The Standard Highway Code quite specifically mentions locations where you should not park your car. Examples are on a blind bend, at the brow of a hill, near a pedestrian crossing, etc, and the Volvo Driver is required to comply with these regulations. However, you could be forgiven for thinking that anywhere else is fair game; after all, it *is* your road. But unfortunately these things are never that straightforward. There are a few other locations where it is NOT advisable to park your Volvo for a variety of reasons. You already have quite a wide choice of parking places available to you (see previous section) so there's little point in deliberately winding up the Peaked Cap Brigade or putting your Volvo at undue risk from wheel-clampers and tow-trucks. For example, you are advised not to park in these places:

- In a disabled space (unless of course you have the appropriate badge). This is about as anti-social as you can get and the Volvo Driver would not want to be associated with such actions.

- In a police station car park. Very tempting since it's one of the few places where your Volvo isn't likely to suffer attempted theft / break-ins or removal of your alloys. However, Mr Plod is not renowned for his magnanimity in allowing Joe Public to share his parking facilities.

- In a Greasy Spoon lorry park, or "Truckstop" as they are affectionately called. If you have been obliged, during the course of your journey, to put one or two lorry drivers in their place *(see section 11)*, a Truckstop is where you stand a good chance of meeting up with them again. This may not be to your advantage.

- Anywhere on a Red Route. These are known to be over-populated with spy cameras and have tow-trucks on demand.

- Anywhere near a football stadium on match days. Your innocently-parked Volvo could attract all sorts of unwanted attention from jubilant fans (winning team), pissed-off fans (losing team), and bored fans (0-0 draw). Hub-caps were designed to protect your wheel hubs from dirt and damage, not to be used as frisbees for terrorising innocent bystanders.

- Anywhere near a school, especially at the beginning or end of the school day. This is when a particularly lethal strain of Woman Driver - the *Woman 4x4 Driver* - takes to the road. Grown men have been reduced to jelly as *Woman 4x4 Driver* emerges from her driveway for the 200-yard dash to school, terrorising other children, old ladies and even Lollipop Persons in her quest to be the closest to the school gates to drop off Chloe and Tristram. This is followed by a manoeuvre lasting approximately half an hour as *Woman 4x4 Driver* then proceeds to pretend she can turn the 4x4 around in a 26-point turn, via walls, trees and other vehicles with a dozen other Woman 4x4 Drivers trying to do exactly the same thing.

- In Town Hall car parks in spaces preciously reserved for the Chairman of the Council, Leader of the Council, Counter of the Paper Clips and other assorted self-appointed bigwigs. These people are ***important*** and take their parking spaces very seriously. They can command legions of jobsworths who can be mobilised at a moment's notice armed with wheel clamps and rolls of parking tickets.

- In what appears to be a temporary car park fashioned out of a demolition site. These are usually run by Del-Boy squatters, out to make a quick buck at renting out parking spaces at exorbitant rates before the rightful owner moves in to chuck them out.

- Across MY driveway.

21.3   How to Park - The techniques involved in parking your Volvo can be considered from two angles; parallel parking and bay parking. Let's look at the specific skills you will need for each:

> 1.   *Parallel parking* - this essentially means along the side of the road between two other parked vehicles. (We will not even consider the option of parking in a clear road since the realistic chances of you finding one are slightly less than spotting Elvis in Sainsbury's). So you locate a space between two parked cars; your next trick will involve manoeuvring your Volvo into it. You shouldn't worry too much if the space isn't quite long enough - with your bumpers, and especially with your tow bar at the back, you will be able to adjust the space to fit your needs. This is why they are called "bumpers". Of course, should your Volvo be of the 4x4 type, equipped with battering ram assemblies of bull-bars and spotlight mountings then your task of adjusting the space to fit will be made that much easier.
>
> Then of course there will always be the occasion when you have managed to find that elusive parking space and parked

up, that you return to find that both of the original cars that you parked between have gone and been replaced by new vehicles, both of which are now parked right up against your bumper(s). Research has shown that this can be due to two reasons:

(1)   Your Volvo has induced jealousy in the other car owners, who have decided to teach you a lesson.

(2)   The other cars are driven by women.

You should not be put to any undue inconvenience and you should use your bumpers to widen the gap to get yourself out. You may also want to commend the other drivers' parking skills and / or take some appropriate retaliatory action for the inconvenience they've caused you, and the following are suggested ways of doing this:

• Leave a note on his / her windscreen, NOT to leave your details so that they can contact you with regards to the damage you may have been obliged to inflict. This is justifiable wear and tear. Instead, thank them for parking so close and tell them that next time you'll bring a tin-opener with you to enable you to extricate yourself that bit easier.

• Take the registration number(s) and either anonymously report the car(s) to the police as stolen, or advertise the car(s) in *AutoTrader*.

2.   *Parking bays* -   referring back to *Dullroy's Laws of Parking*, and in particular to Law 6, the space allocated per car does not only refer to the length of the car but also to the width. Nowhere is this more evident than in local council pay-and-display car parks where spaces are marked out in bays.

Some councils work on the principle that the more cars they can cram into their parking lots, the more revenue they can extract from the captive motorists. It therefore follows that each bay will be as compact (i.e. small) as possible. This may be fine when the cars are Minis or Micras, but absolutely no consideration has been given to Volvos. How many times have you found a parking space in a municipal car park, having just spent three hours looking for it, only to find that if you park in it you'll have to get out through the sunroof? The Town Hall muppets just couldn't care less, so you should treat them and their measly parking spaces with the same contempt. You pays your money so you're entitled to park your car and at least be able to get out of it easily without putting your back out. You need the space to move so you should think nothing of parking so close to the white lines of one of the parking bays that nobody else could realistically use the spare bay. This is just a little bit more subtle than ostentatiously parking centrally across two bays, always assuming of course that you're ever going to find two empty bays together. Of course, should you feel the need to make a point then park centrally across two bays. Or go for a cluster and park over the corners of four bays, safe in the knowledge that nobody will dare to leave so much as a fingerprint on your Volvo.

With respect to paying for your parking you would be wise to have on your person a wide selection of coins to feed the pay-and-display meter when you park, and a wad of readies to pay those nice gentlemen to take the clamp off your front wheel when you return.

22.   ROAD WORKS:

The most successful and widespread growth industry in Britain today. If ever the enterprising Volvo Driver wanted to earn himself a small fortune by diversifying his commercial expertise he could do a lot worse than rent a unit factory, buy a couple of re-conditioned plastics extrusion machines, and make traffic cones. Whereas it is accepted that the roads the Volvo Driver uses should be kept in a good state of repair the sheer number and scale of road works on the go at any one time these days leads to a deep underlying suspicion that a lot of it exists purely as job creation exercises. Whatever, it is an inescapable fact that, for once, the Volvo Driver has something in common with every other road user (wheeled ones, that is). Road Works are an expanding industry and contribute to making any journey as frustrating as possible. They spring up under all sorts of disguises, and are controlled in all sorts of ways; coned-off lanes, contraflows, temporary traffic lights, and even stout yeomen with red and green STOP / GO signs.

22.1   The Causes of Road Works - Road Works can appear at a moment's notice and for any number of reasons. Here is a selection which I'm sure you'll be familiar with:

> 1.   *Actual repairs / re-surfacing* - the road surface that was originally laid to accommodate Volvos and other cars has been wrecked by the increasing numbers of 44-tonne trucks, car transporters, Boris and his Eastern European juggernauts etc, and needs to be replaced.

> 2.   *Emergency hole-digging* - the water main has burst - not a lot you can do about this.

> 3.   *Non-emergency hole-digging:*

>> -   the gas companies decide to lay new pipes; *but NOT at the same time as:*

>> -   the water companies who decide to lay new pipes; *but NOT at the same time as:*

-    the electric companies who decide to renew their cabling; *but NOT at the same time as:*

-    the telephone companies who decide to renew their cabling; *but NOT at the same time as:*

-    the cable TV companies who decide to install their wiring systems.

The eventual result is a patchwork quilt of tarmac, all laid at different levels, designed to test the suspension struts of the hardiest of cars when driven over them. Fortunately, your Volvo will be equal to the task.

4.   *Grass cutting and / or hedge trimming*   - not Road Works as such, but the authorities still deem it necessary to cone off miles of carriageway lanes in order to protect a single tractor or mower working on the verges, slowly inching its way along. Its progress can be measured in days rather than hours.

5.   *Erecting / replacing barriers on central reservations* - many dual carriageways have been built without protective barriers along the central reservation. After the first 20 or 30 fatal cross-over crashes the Highways Agency decides that it's probably a good idea to erect the barriers that should have been put up when the road was being built. Either that, or the barriers they did put up were purely cosmetic, i.e. served no useful purpose, and now need to be replaced by the genuine article. This will entail coning off the fast lanes for weeks on end and naturally since only a few hundred yards of barrier can be erected at any one time you will find that the entire stretch to be worked (about five miles) will be coned off in one go.

6.   *Bridge repairs* - a bridge across or under a road is only a few yards wide. It will therefore be necessary to cone off two miles of your road in each direction to accommodate this.

7.   *Building new roads / motorways / intersections* - even the Volvo Driver can't complain too much about delays and frustrations arising from any attempts to improve the road system that he uses. After all, if you want the rainbow you have to put up with the rain. No point in being churlish, even if some of the Road Works do seem to be a permanent feature to the point that they appear on the next editions of your local Ordnance Survey map.

8.   *Painting markings on roads (1)* - this is not just painting or re-painting white lines down the centre of the road, or lane markings on motorways. This is necessary because, though the Volvo Driver instinctively knows what side of the road or which lane he should be using, to lesser mortals this often causes confusion. Guidance in the form of white lines is therefore essential. But unfortunately road painting isn't limited to this. There is now the latest fashion for painting the road in pretty colours. The old-style black tarmac with white lines and cats eyes is now so un-cool. Decoration is therefore required to emphasise what any normal person would view as the bleedin' obvious. So be prepared for great swathes of coned-off road lanes set aside for the local council to display their hitherto untapped artistic talents for your appreciation. The resulting works of art can include the following:

(1)   Dual carriageway lanes painted across with yellow stripes for the preceding half mile before a roundabout. This is obviously to alert the Volvo Driver who cannot read the great big green and white sign, followed by a local black and white sign, informing motorists of the

approaching roundabout and the directions available.

(2)   Painting the town (or country) red - the latest fad for painting great blocks of the road surface in a gaudy brick-red colour:

• like the yellow stripes above, you will now find large red stripes across the road as you approach a village or road junction on a dual carriageway;

• widening the centre of the road, narrowing the traffic lanes in the process, painting double sets of dotted white lines in the middle, then filling the gap between these lines with red paint as an indication that you can't use it. Presumably, adding an extra lane instead to keep the traffic flowing is too easy.

• painting whole bus lanes red.

(3)   Adding to the colourful scene by painting cycle lanes in a nice shade of green *(see also section 3)*. At traffic lights these suddenly spread out at right angles to cover your half of the road in a big green rectangle. This is to allow cyclists to assume the positions of a Formula 1 starting grid waiting for the lights to change while everybody else queues obediently behind them.

As a result of all this you could find yourself in a city centre driving on a road that has more colours than a kiddy's paint box. Reading from the kerb to the centre of the road there will be a bus or "no car" lane in brick red edged by a white line, then the green bike lane again edged in white, and then what's left of your half of the road finished in a dreamy bog-standard black tarmac. This will occasionally be interspersed with the yellow hatchings of a box junction.

It doesn't stop with dividing the road up into pretty coloured stripes, either. In some towns, just when you thought you had a bit of road all to yourself, you find that the area at the centre of the road is occupied by tram lines, thus diminishing still further the amount of road available to you. This has been known to induce a type of road rage, and whereas you may be tempted to dispute ownership of a bike lane with a lone cyclist, trying to contest territorial superiority with a tram is unwise, even in a Volvo.

9.   *Painting markings on roads (2)* - painting a continuous pattern of pretty chevrons on the road surface on all the lanes of a motorway, e.g. the M6. It is widely thought that this is to tell you how far apart you should be driving from the vehicle in front - two chevrons should always be visible between you. This is of exceptional value in conditions of driving rain or fog where you're lucky to be able to see the front of your Volvo, much less fancy patterns on the road surface sixty feet in front. Also, you will find that this rule only applies to vehicles under two tonnes, as you discover when the sky behind your Volvo suddenly darkens with a car transporter breathing down your neck. In such cases you will need to take appropriate action to remind this car transporter of his position in life *(see section 11.6 for details)*.

In actual fact, these road markings are not chevrons at all but double "V"s which of course indicate that the lanes these are painted on are for Volvos only. They should therefore only ever appear in the outside lanes of motorways, but in predictable fashion the Equality Police have decided that this would discriminate against lesser car users so they paint them in every lane.

22.2   The 15 Laws of Road Works - We saw in the previous section on parking that there are some fundamental laws of nature which come into play, based upon the Law of Sod. Unfortunately you will find that there are similar laws governing Road Works, and at some time or another the Volvo Driver will become their hapless victim. Fate has decreed it to be so. These are ***Dullroy's Fifteen Laws of Road Works*** and these are listed below:

Law 1:   *Where two miles of road need to be repaired, coned-off lanes or a contraflow will extend for six miles.*

Law 2:   *Contraflow lanes marked with luminous yellow studs are slightly too narrow for your car and become excellent features for removing wing mirrors.*

Law 3:   *The length of coned-off lanes is inversely proportional to the amount of work actually being carried out in them.*

Law 4:   *Dual carriageway lanes are always coned-off just as you reach them, having been stuck behind a tractor / JCB / Caravan / Sunday Driver for the last ten miles and the dual carriageway offers the first opportunity to overtake.*

Law 5:   *You will not see a tractor / JCB / Caravan / Sunday Driver for miles until you enter a single lane contraflow which extends for six miles.*

Law 6:   *The "sorry for any delay" signs that greet you at the end of a contraflow will have a speed camera hidden behind it just as you leg it out of the Road Works but before the speed de-restriction sign.*

Law 7:   *The persons responsible for the "sorry for any delay"*

164

signs are not sorry for any delay. Delays are their mission in life.

Law 8:   *The Cones Hotline (??) is always engaged.*

Law 9:   *On the rare occasion that you do manage to get through to the Cones Hotline you will encounter an answering machine.*

Law 10:   *The miles and miles of coned-off fast lane on a dual carriageway ends abruptly with no obstacles and no sign of any Road Works activities, so you could have driven down it anyway.*

Law 11:   *Had you done so you would have screamed round a bend to be confronted by the one gigantic piece of tarmac-laying equipment actually in use that day. Either that or a jam sandwich parked up with its occupants having their lunch.*

Law 12:   *Cones are always on your side of the dual carriageway and never on the other. On your return journey they will have been switched across.*

Law 13:   *The most inaccessible part of the Road Works will be designated as a tow-truck recovery zone for breakdowns, statutory removal fee £75.*

Law 14:   *This is where you will have your only puncture in two years.*

Law 15:   *When the Road Works have been completed, the contraflow system dismantled, and the road returns to normal, the temporary "50 mph" and speed camera signs will be left in place for at least another two months.*

23.   THE VOLVO DRIVER AND MR PLOD:

From what we've established so far we can say, without any fear of contradiction, that you - the Volvo Driver - are an exclusive breed. You have been thoroughly instructed in your very own Highway Code. You are superior to all other road users and you have been taught to drive in a manner befitting this philosophy; i.e. you are never in the wrong, your journey is the most important, and rules and regulations just get in the way. It is, however, an inescapable fact of life that these views are not always shared with the rest of the motoring fraternity, and in particular the law. It is therefore inevitable that at some point you will cross swords with Mr Plod the Policeman.

During the course of this book we have already mentioned Mr Plod many times, and in particular the mobile Mr Plod in his jam sandwich *(section 5.9)* and in his more sinister disguise as an unmarked car *(section 5.10)*. However, at this point we thought it would be useful to summarise some of the other ways in which the Volvo Driver may come into contact with HM Constabulary during the course of his journey, and what he should (or shouldn't) do in each case.

Let's start first with an introduction to try and establish the role of the modern mobile Mr Plod so that the Volvo Driver can gain a better appreciation of what to expect. Appropriately, we will call this *"Losing the Plot"*. Other sections follow:

23.1   Losing the Plot - The original purpose of Mr Plod, the Highway Patroller, was to exert some form of stabilising influence on standards of driving and motoring. He could appear on point duty directing traffic, or be seen cruising up and down the highways in his little panda car. He was available for help and advice, and if a ticking off for a minor traffic transgression was considered necessary he would administer it. There was an ethos (albeit somewhat strained sometimes) of mutual respect. But that was then and, as the Volvo Driver knows only too well, the modern face of the law presents a totally different image. It is fairly safe to say that 21st century Mr Plod has lost the plot. He is no longer there to advise, warn, or generally assist the motorist. He is there to screw the motorist, and as many as possible, in order to achieve targets set for speeding and other minor traffic offences by politically correct Chief Constables. Mr Plod's prime purpose in life is to fill in forms, attend courses on racial awareness and seminars on sexual discrimination in the workplace, and set up traps to catch Volvo Drivers slipping into a bus lane, or doing 32mph in a built-up area. Actual crime just gets in the way of modern policing. These, then, are the underlying philosophies facing the Volvo Driver. Now, read on.....

23.2   Police Stopping Procedure - There is a formal procedure which Mr Plod will use if he wants to pull you over for a chat. The Standard Highway Code defines this as the "Police Stopping Procedure"; the *Volvo Driver's Highway Code* defines it as the "Police Harassment Procedure". This will inevitably involve the use of all of Mr Plod's red and blue roof lights, flashing headlights, and probably his siren as well, depending upon his frame of mind. After all, he needs to make an impression. After a lengthy discussion in the back of his jam sandwich, painstakingly inspecting your driving licence, trying to smell your breath and delivering a patronising lecture on the finer points of traffic law, he solemnly informs you that the reason he stopped you was because one of the screws in your back licence plate is not in regulation yellow, is therefore the wrong colour, and is a threat to national security.

23.3   WPC Plod - Occasionally, the boys in blue may raise the stakes a little and unleash their secret weapon on you - WPC Plod, the lady police constable. Now, just pause for a moment to reflect on this fearsome hybrid of a Woman Driver and Mr Plod. Now factor in a hefty helping of PMT and the end result doesn't bear thinking about. Unfortunately they do exist and if you come into contact with one you are recommended to show due deference. Try and resist the temptation to greet her with *"Hello! Hello! Hello!"* or suggest some interesting, if unorthodox, alternative uses for her handcuffs. After all, she may call your bluff and you really don't want to add further delays to your journey by having to go to the nearest Accident & Emergency Department so that she can get her truncheon back.

23.4   The Covert Operation - Another effective way of utilising precious police resources in the fight against the rising tide of crime is the "fuzztrap". This is a covert operation involving three, four, five or even seven police officers who will be stationed behind a bush or somebody's front garden wall awaiting the arrival of a speeding motorist, or a Volvo Driver performing a right turn into a road that has been a right of way for yonks but has now been designated "No Right Turn". At a given signal they leap out and surround the hapless driver who will now probably be criminalised for this infringement. Meanwhile, a quarter of a mile up the road, burglars, muggers and car thieves are having a field day.

23.5   The Sitting Target - If you think that you're only vulnerable to Mr Plod when you're on the move, think again. He can also get you when you're stationary. This can be for a number of reasons, such as:

- Waiting for you to park on a yellow line for 30 seconds while you nip out to buy a newspaper from a street seller.

- Waiting for you to pull up at traffic lights and spots you unwrapping a chocolate while you wait for the lights to change.

- Giving your Volvo the quick once-over for possible tax disc infringements, looking for a dud bulb in your lights, or estimating the depth of tread on your tyres.

- Waiting for you to park and pouncing on you for parking slightly out of the parking bay.

23.6   The Road Block - Setting up a road block is an effective way for Mr Plod to make his presence felt. This will enable him to stop and search any motorist at any time and for any reason, which totally countermands the old democratic system of needing a good reason for bothering you. These days *The Prevention of Terrorism Act* is all they need. If you are stopped in this fashion you should challenge them and ask, politely but firmly, why you have been pulled over. They may offer plausible reasons, or they may not, but if they do they will be along the following lines:

- They're running a joint undercover exercise with Customs & Excise looking for contraband booze and fags.

- They're looking for asylum seekers hidden in the boot of your Volvo.

- A car answering the description of your Volvo (and probably dozens of others) ran a red light back in town - yesterday.

- A driver of a Volvo answering your description was caught on camera driving without the requisite two hands on the steering wheel, and a county-wide search has been instigated.

And so it goes on. Now, the Volvo Driver is not stupid. He knows that the real reasons he has been stopped are likely to be:

(1)   Divisional HQ have told mobile Mr Plods to up their quotas for persecuting motorists for having up-side down tax disks, number plates with the characters in the wrong typeface, and windows made out of dark glass that can render the driver invisible to a speed camera.

(2)   Using any of these reasons as a pretence, and while they're doing this they will be performing contortions to smell your breath for tell-tale signs of inappropriate liquid refreshment.

(3)   They are bored out of their tiny minds (not difficult).

23.7   The Spy in the Sky - It's not just on the ground that you have to worry about Mr Plod. Just when you thought it was safe to put your S60R through its paces Mr Plod comes up with yet another innovative way of frustrating you. You have found yourself a nice quiet stretch of country road where it is entirely possible that you may, through a careless oversight, exceed the permitted speed limit by a few mph. Since you are miles from anywhere with no jam sandwich or speed camera in sight you may feel that this is a risk worth taking. This is when the boys in blue play their trump card and instead of attacking on the ground suddenly descend on you from a great height in a helicopter. Yes, a helicopter - and not just any helicopter. Most police forces have one these days for spotting and pursuing vagabonds, but these are special Traffic Enforcement Helicopters equipped with radar guns - a sort of Noddy helicopter gunship, if you like. Upwards of half a million pounds of taxpayer's money dedicated to enforcing speed limits on deserted open roads. Wonderful stuff. Now, the Volvo Driver would do well to remember this and plan accordingly:

●   Noddy gunships make a hell of a racket, so it should be possible to hear one before it fixes you in its sights. Just don't drive with the stereo system too loud.

●   You've just found another use for your glass sunroof *(see section 17.9)*. This will give you added aerial vision to help you to detect visible signs of helicopter activity. However, persistently looking through your sunroof while speed testing an S60R is not recommended.

23.8   Have Camera, Will Travel - Let's refer back to our section on speed cameras *(18.4.2)*. Mr Plod maintains that speed cameras are only sited at "accident blackspots" to improve road safety. The Volvo Driver knows this to be a crock of crap. Well, at the time of writing we are given to understand that every "accident blackspot" now has a

170

speed camera which means that the use of these cameras has reached saturation point. This has given Mr Plod a problem. He needs to increase the revenue from his speeding fines to meet his targets and the only way he can now do this is to site more cameras in other locations. If he does this will confirm to a sceptical motoring public what they've known all along - i.e. that speed cameras are all about making lots of lovely money for the authorities rather than saving lives. Mr Plod is therefore between a rock and a hard place but never, ever, underestimate his ability to come up with a cunning plan. This time it's the *Mobile Speed Camera*. So all he has to do is to keep the stationary cameras where they are and put extra cameras in unmarked jam sandwiches. He can then drive around the country unnoticed and set up secret speed traps wherever he likes. Mr Plod in Dreamland.

Knowing the mentality of our law enforcers the Volvo Driver will not be surprised by this latest assault on his human rights and will probably wonder why Mr Plod hadn't thought of it before. So if you end up on the wrong end of a Mobile Speed Camera you should proceed as we described in section 18.4.2.

Discussion Point: We all know about the targets that Mr Plod is given for nailing motorists for all manner of trivial offences; this is beyond dispute. But has anybody ever heard of targets set by Chief Constables for apprehending burglars, muggers, car thieves and other low-lifes? No, nor have I.

23.9   The Lone Ranger - Mr Plod likes to travel alone because he can get up to all sorts of tricks without anybody checking up on him. Being paid by results (convictions) he knows this. He won't go looking for street crime in case he finds some and gets hurt, or some nasty person shouts at him, so he heads for the evergreen soft option; the motorist.

One of Mr Plod's favourite stunts is to lurk in the vicinity of petrol station forecourts. As you drive your Volvo into the garage and head for your chosen petrol pump **Mr Plod** will be waiting to see if you unclip your seat belt before you actually roll to a halt. Should you be reckless enough to do so you will find yourself £30 the poorer as **Mr Plod** notches up another "result" with which to ingratiate himself with his section commander. Of course, should you suggest to **Mr Plod** that he is outside his jurisdiction as the garage forecourt is private property then be prepared to face the full might of the law as you are breathalysed, your Volvo painstakingly checked for tax discs, tyre treads, and bulbs in good working order, and your Volvo's boot is inspected to ensure that it doesn't contain contraband anti-tank missiles or anything else that takes his fancy. Your response to this infringement of your civil liberties is to announce your intention of checking *his* Noddy car for proper tax, tyre treads, and dud bulbs etc with a view to making a citizen's arrest. See how he likes it.

Note of Caution: If you do intend to check his car out make sure you have a passenger with you to corroborate your actions. But then again, if you weren't on your own **Mr Plod** wouldn't have pulled you in the first place.

23.10   PC Putt-Putt; The Yellow Peril - What is it with reflective plastic yellow jackets? They seem to have this uncanny ability to turn what was once a reasonable person into the *Jobsworth From Hell*. There you are, motoring along in your Volvo and minding your own business when you encounter a Lollipop Person *(see section 18.11.2)* doing her stuff. Dressed in a reflective plastic yellow jacket. Once you've escaped her clutches you then try and find somewhere to park for a minute while you nip out to buy your morning paper, only to find that your chosen parking place is being patrolled by a Traffic Warden on red alert. Dressed in a reflective plastic yellow jacket. The municipal car park is also a non-starter; this is under the watchful eye of the Car-Clamping Gestapo. Dressed in reflective plastic yellow jackets.

All this does little to put you in the right frame of mind to continue your journey but because these delays have combined to make you late you push on regardless. You will be keeping your usual look-out for Mr Plod and all is well - until you carelessly nudge 42 mph in that urban 40 mph zone. This is when you realise Mr Plod has been with you all the time - riding a motorbike and hiding in the blind spot in your offside wing mirror, just waiting for the opportunity to pounce. Dressed in a reflective plastic yellow jacket. Well, I never. Mr Plod on two wheels. PC Putt-Putt, no less. At this point he switches on his siren and little blue flashing lights and proceeds to pull you over for the inevitable bollocking and speeding ticket. This is when you notice he's wearing jackboots with his reflective yellow jacket. This is essential for him to really look the part.

Now, PC Putt-Putt is a versatile servant of the law. For example he can be:

- a motorcycle outrider for a wide load on a motorway;

- an escort for VIPs as they sweep along bus lanes in their limos;

- a leader of a gang of PC Putt-Putts hanging around on motorway bridges to unsettle the traffic below;

- a reinforcement for Mr Plod in his jam sandwich, reaching those parts Mr Plod can't reach; for example, chasing wrong-doers up alleyways.

He can also be a pain in the arse. Literally. If you are unfortunate enough to be pulled by PC Putt-Putt you should really do your best to keep calm. Rumour has it that riding a motorbike all day gives PC Putt-Putt a sore bum so he's likely to be on a short fuse. Best not to unduly aggravate him. For example, you are advised to refrain from asking him if his pizzas aren't getting cold while he's detaining you, or asking for his autograph since you're sure you saw him in a repeat of

"Colditz" on *UK Gold* the other night.

24.   CONCLUSION - The End of your Journey:

And there you have it. Everything you've always wanted to know about driving your Volvo but were afraid to ask. I hope that this book has contributed in some small way to making your journey that bit more bearable. Remember that your journey is going to be fraught with challenges and problems (some may say opportunities) form the minute you get into your Volvo, start the engine and slip the handbrake. You are technically, socially and morally superior to everybody else on the road but you will find that this isn't a view that's widely shared by other road users. They don't like you because you've got something they haven't got - a Volvo. And deep-down they know that you're also a better driver, and they can't deal with that, either. Your journey is always important and you will always have a tight schedule, but unfortunately you will find that you are the only person on the roads that understands this. The authorities, with their regulations and incessant nannying, combine to hinder, obstruct and harass you at every available opportunity. What they fail to appreciate is that their rules and regulations are only there as ***guidelines***, to be interpreted for your specific purposes to ensure that your journey is completed to schedule and with the minimum of hassle.

As a consequence of all this the Volvo Driver could be forgiven for wondering why the hell he bothers, but he has a duty that cannot be ignored. He is there to set an example; to establish the Volvo Driver at the forefront of motoring; to set the standards for others to follow. And to achieve this feathers will have to be ruffled, egos deflated and noses put out of joint as society struggles to come to terms with it all. Shame really, but they'll get over it. However it does mean that you, as the Volvo Driver, are setting yourself up as the motorist's public enemy number one, which is reflected in the inevitable outbursts of *"Bloody Volvo Drivers!"* as you cruise past on the outside lane of the motorway. You'll just have to grit your teeth and dig your heels in - they're only jealous. Remember:

"Just because you refuse to be paranoiac about everybody else on the road doesn't mean to say they're not out to get you!"

Enjoy your Volvo!

Part C: SIGNALS & SIGNS

This part of the *Volvo Driver's Highway Code* deals with the use and interpretation of signals to be used by the Volvo Driver, and the road signs that he will encounter on his travels.

25. HAND SIGNALS:

Much as it goes against the grain, there **will** be occasions when the Volvo Driver will need to employ signals to let other road users know of his intentions, and perhaps to convey other messages. These signals are in addition to the usual direction indicators and are normally given by hand. The following are four specific examples of hand signals which can be used by the Volvo Driver, and an interpretation of what each is intended to convey:

Thank you for holding me up
for the last twenty miles with
your caravan

Thank you for showering me
with all that mud from your
tractor's wheels

God bless you, Mr Truck Driver

I have formed a very low
opinion of your driving ability

26.   ROAD SIGNS:

The Standard Highway Code classifies road signs into *Warning Signs*, *Signs Giving Orders*, and *Direction Signs*. Oh yes, and they also have a special category for Road Works called, would you believe, *Road Works Signs*. Who said Road Works weren't here to stay?

The meaning of each sign is listed in the Standard Highway Code. However, the Volvo Driver has a entirely different perception for his purposes, and the whole concept of *Warning Signs*, *Signs Giving Orders*, and *Direction Signs* take on a whole new meaning. Oh yes, almost forgot; so do *Road Works Signs*. On the next pages you will find a wide selection of the most common road signs, and how these are interpreted by the Volvo Driver:

Drive in both directions at once direction

You've just gone in the wrong

Viagra factory ahead

No swearing

Welcome to Transylvania

Drunk drivers only

Launderette ahead

Nudist colony ahead

Volvo drivers parking

Women drivers parking

Inferior car factory ahead

Maternity hospital ahead

Unfriendly local residents

20% chance of making it

Cemetery ahead

Mother-in-law's house ahead

Scrapyard ahead

Welcome to Cambridge

Volvos have priority on the right

Jaywalker catchment area

Underground car park

Do not anger the Gods

Man opening umbrella

Cyclists not welcome

Cambridge is full - go home

Stunt riders only

Another 6 penalty points

Outside toilets ahead

Toilets ahead

Toilets open Saturdays only

HEAVY PLANT CROSSING

Fat (sorry, calorifically challenged) people should proceed with caution

It's that oak tree again

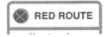

Manchester United supporters only

Part D: A BRIEF GLOSSARY OF TERMS USED IN THIS BOOK

Listed below you will find a brief glossary of some of the terms and expressions used in this book which we hope will assist you in your interpretation of the *Volvo Driver's Highway Code:*

Abnormal Load   Mobile road block.

Aquaplaning   The art of driving on the surface of water. Eliminates the need to steer.

Artic   Very large articulated vehicle such as a container lorry or a car transporter.

Black Ice   Meteorological feature for turning Volvos into scrap metal. Politically incorrect skidpan.

Boy Racer   Adolescent driver with Formula One ambitions. Easily distinguishable by back-to-front baseball cap.

Bus Lane   Express thoroughfare for buses, coaches and government ministers late for appointments.

Cambridge   Cyclists' nesting ground.

Clamp   A device that's fitted to a vehicle that's causing an obstruction to ensure that it stays there.

Coffin-dodger   Elderly driver on borrowed time.

Cone, Traffic

An alien life form that multiplies by binary fission under cover of darkness.

Congestion Charge

Mr Livingstone's *"Welcome to London. Have a nice day"*. Gridlock tax.

Contraflow

Temporary carriageways constructed within long-term Road Works where traffic in both directions uses one side of a motorway. A horizontal Wall of Death.

Cyclist

Rudimentary life-form on 2-wheeled transportation.

Fun Run

Sponsored gridlock of main trunk roads by hordes of jogging, wheezing pedestrians, very few of which are actually having any fun.

Fuzztrap

Stake-out involving a whole squad of Old Bill playing with their radar guns.

Girl Racer

As for Boy Racer, but without the cap. Usually with the added benefit of PMT (see PMT).

Greasy Spoon

Roadside catering establishment specialising in good wholesome home cooking for the man on the move.

Gridlock

Impromptu parking lot. The Volvo Driver's nemesis.

Jam Sandwich

Police patrol car. Plodmobile.

Jaywalker

Absent-minded pedestrian with a death wish.

JCB

The leading vehicle in a 6-mile contraflow. An abbreviation of **J**amming **C**ountry **B**yways.

Jogger

Ultra-mobile pedestrian with a death wish.

Learner Driver

Student of the **H**ighways **I**n **T**raining. Usually abbreviated to S.H.I.T.

Level Crossing

Where road meets railway. A rare opportunity for the Volvo Driver to eat humble pie.

Lollipop Person

Geriatric guardian of the nation's schoolchildren. A troll in a reflective yellow plastic jacket.

Mr Plod

Representative of the local constabulary. Old Bill. Fuzz. Piggy-wig.

Noddy

Mr Plod.

Noddy Gunship

Police helicopter dedicated to "traffic enforcement" duties.

Oak Tree

A plant that grows in the same spot for 700 years and then suddenly jumps out in front of a woman driver.

Parking

The ultimate challenge for women drivers. *("I can do it when you're not looking, so sod off")*.

Plonker

Person of dubious driving ability. Fool. Lunatic. Nutcase. Meathead. Dork. Nimrod.

PMT

Hormonal catalyst that transforms a placid lady driver into the psycho-bitch from hell.

Rat Run

Back street speedway. Used to avoid congested main roads.

Road Rage

Psychotic condition induced by the dawning realisation of the superiority of the Volvo Driver.

SIPS

Volvo's own *Side Impact Protection System* designed to minimise injuries caused by a plonker driving into the side of your car. See "plonker" above.

Speed Camera

A licence for Mr Plod to print money.

Sunday Driver

Slow-witted individual with no sense of awareness. Flat cap fanatic.

T5

A Volvo with attitude.

Tailgating	The art of driving close enough to the car in front so that you can see the whites of the other driver's eyes in his rear view mirror.
Tractor	The farmer's revenge.
Traffic Warden	Pond life in uniform. A challenge when parking your Volvo.
Torture Bells	Volvo's way of telling you to belt up.
Unmarked Police Car	A dirty rotten trick.
Volvo Driver	Simply the best.
White Van Man	Neanderthal throwback.
Wheel Clamp	see *Clamp*
Woman Driver	God's little joke.
Woman 4X4 Driver	God's little joke in armour plating.
Woman Volvo Driver	Your worst nightmare
WPC Plod	Female representative of the local constabulary. Mr Plod with PMT.

PEFC Certified

This product is
from sustainably
managed forests
and controlled
sources

www.pefc.org

PEFC/16-33-415

Reprint of # - C8 - 210/148/10 - PB - Lamination Gloss - Printed on 09-Mar-18 16:31